Between Two Worlds
- A Narrative

Shirla Philogène

authorHOUSE®

AuthorHouse™ UK Ltd.
500 Avebury Boulevard
Central Milton Keynes, MK9 2BE
www.authorhouse.co.uk
Phone: 08001974150

First published by AuthorHouse 10/1/2008

ISBN: 978-1-4389-1155-7 (sc)
ISBN: 978-1-4389-1156-4 (hc)

Printed in the United States of America
Bloomington, Indiana

This book is printed on acid-free paper.

This book is dedicated to the memory of my three sisters and brother
The Late Pauline-Allen-Young, The Late Ercelle Allen-Cummings
The Late Lorna Allen-Small
and
The Late George Lipton Eardlie Allen

They encouraged me to go to school

Shirla Philogène was born and educated in St Vincent and the Grenadines. She arrived in England to pursue a career in nursing. She currently lives in North London. This is her first publication.

Table of Contents

My World as a Child

I thought the earth was the true universe
That it was a beautiful place
And moon, sun, and stars belonged to it.

I thought heaven was behind the sky
And the sky was earth's roof, painted blue,
That the moon became the sun at night
To make the darkness light.

I thought that breeze was the air we breathed
And it was pure.
I thought heaven opened its doors
To send rain upon the earth
To make plants grow
And flowers bloom.

I thought oceans were blue
That they met at the horizon
And mountains touched the sky

Chapter 1:
Early Childhood

St Vincent, the 18 × 11 mile West Indian island so often excluded from maps of the world, is my homeland. It is special. It belongs to me and I belong to it. My island is volcanic and forms part of the Windward Island group. It lies approximately 100 miles west of Barbados and 170 miles north of Trinidad, and it is referred to as the Gem of the Antilles.

Kingstown, the capital, is situated to the south-eastern corner of the island. The harbour is sheltered between Old Woman's Point and Cane Garden. One of the most breathtaking scenes ever to be captured from the vantage point of a ship's deck is the early-morning sun rising over the harbour.

The village where I grew up lies on the Windward side; it is approximately three-quarters of a mile long and is wedged between the red cliffs and the sea, or as the villagers called it, the Bluff and the Bay side. The Atlantic Ocean washes the windward coast. The sea is rough, the coastline rugged. Black sandy beaches, a feature of volcanic islands, join huge black rocks that jut out of the sea and mountainous waves that splash against the rocks sending sprays high into the surrounding atmosphere, to create a scene that is frighteningly dramatic.

And yet I was not afraid, for our house was built along the Bay side, where the shore was covered for a quarter of a mile with stones and boulders, not sand. I claimed it as an extension of our yard. The stones and boulders were my friends. I hid behind them and climbed on top of them. I was their teacher. They were my pupils. I flogged them when they made me fall. I plaited their green mossy hair. They were my real playmates. I think they knew that. I liked them, and they in turn liked me. Life for my imaginary friends and for me was magical and full of fun when I was 4 years old.

The sea and its tide produced its own peculiar magic, at least so it seemed tome This magic appeared three or four times a year and brought with, it delight and restriction. Delight because on waking in the morning I found that during the night, the strong Atlantic tide had played a trick on me and covered the entire beach with shining black sand. Restriction because my playmates were hidden, and other children from the neighbourhood invaded my territory, intruded into my extended playing field, and forced my parents to restrict my freedom to wander along the seashore. I was always delighted when the sand disappeared and my imaginary friends became visible once more.

But the stones and boulders were not the only inhabitants of my extended yard. They shared the territory with grape trees that formed natural breakers along the beach and provided protection against the strong winds and the Atlantic waves. Their thick, heart-shaped green leaves, arranged like cupped hands on the branches, were there to shield the purple grapes that had a uniquely salty-sweet taste. Then there were also the taller-than-average coconut palms interspersed amongst the grape trees. These stood bold, erect, and strong, like stalwart giants forming an alliance to protect their domain. Yet there were times when even this alliance supported by the resistance of the rocks and stones fell prey to the relentless onslaught of the Atlantic in the frenzy of a hurricane. It was in those moments that our home and the village became exposed to the ravages of the sea.

Our house was built in 1913, the year my father was married. And, although the building is now much smaller than it had been the date is still inscribed on the outer wall. It was a two-storied house and had an outer staircase of eighteen steps with banisters on either side. These were made from pitch pine and varnished to protect them from the sprays of the sea. As a child I got great pleasure from sliding down these banisters whenever the grownups were out of sight, and from time to time, I would fall on the stony ground below.

Downstairs, there was the shop and the store whose entrance faced the main road, whilst the dining room and pantry had an entrance that faced the sea. Upstairs, there were the bedrooms and the drawing room that had window seats where I stood each day to wave to passers-by and the passengers in the buses on their way to Kingstown. There was a round centre table. During the day it hosted a vase with flowers, but at night a gas lamp became its guest. The lamp provided the light for the room and acted as a beacon for travellers as they passed through the village. Then there was the gallery, with a window that overlooked the sea, where I spent many hours dreaming that one day I would travel to a place where the ocean met the sky.

The kitchen was a separate building with a clay-built oven that my mother used for baking bread and cakes at weekends. The horse stable stood apart from the main building and provided shelter for the horse that was father's means of transport to and from Root Valley, our estate that was situated in Dunbar, some three miles inland. Father inherited Root Valley from his father in 1903, and it still remains in the family.

My father was married twice. His first wife died whilst giving birth to their fourth child. This child also died, and he was left with three others – Earl, aged 5, Elsa, aged 7, and Pearl, aged 9. Relatives rallied around the children, and they were sent to live with an uncle who had an estate on the Leeward end of the island. This was some distance from their father's home on the Windward side, which made it difficult for him to spend time with them.

My father missed his children, so he employed a mature woman of good repute to be a permanent housekeeper. This enabled him to bring them home.

During their time with their uncle, Pearl assumed a measure of responsibility for her younger brother and sister. Many years later, Earl was heard to say, "In those days I didn't realise that Pearl was only a few years older than me. I always did as I was told and never argued." In fact, no one ever argued with her.

Six years after his first wife died, my father married my mother. In the next twelve years, six of us were born, and we became a family of nine. My mother's and Pearl's relationship was like that of big sisters who held each other in high regard and with mutual respect. The words *step* and *half* were not part of our vocabulary, and Pearl, who later became a qualified teacher, assumed the role of authority over the younger siblings and set the boundaries with the tacit consent of our mother. We accepted this as the natural order of things and were disciplined but happy.

I was the third of the new offspring, and up to the age of 4 years, I was allowed a certain amount of freedom, but my other two sisters, who were attending the school where Pearl taught, were firmly under her wings. Each morning the three of them went off together, whilst I stood on the window seat and waved them goodbye before turning my attention to the passengers on the buses going in to the town. I was happy and carefree.

I was not yet 5 years old when I went to Kingstown for the first time with my father. My hair was washed, my church shoes were cleaned, and with a new pair of white socks and a new dress, I was ready for the journey. I was excited and apprehensive. Father had never taken any of his children to Kingstown before, so this was going to be a new experience for him as well.

Father was a farmer. He went to Kingstown at the end of each month and travelled by the mail bus. Mr Carlton, the owner of the bus, knew that. He also knew that my father would not be ready, that he would have to wait, and that his passengers would grumble good-naturedly.

Mr Carlton was an Indian man, jovial, a chain smoker, and small in stature. He enjoyed banter in equal measure to smoking the local brand of Empire cigarettes. On the occasions he was kept waiting, he would turn off the engine, swing his legs over to the side of the bus, and light up. With eyes half closed, he would draw deeply on his cigarette, lift his shoulders, and expand his chest as if he were inhaling the unpolluted sea air.

His passengers, on the other hand, would from time to time shout, "Mr Carlton, what time you think we go reach town today?"

"We always the l-a r-s-t bus to reach Market Square. Time we reach there everything done sell out."

"Mi-sa-ar Allen n-a-a-r going to buy anything. He only going to Bank."

"Mi-sa-ar Carlton, next time Mi-sa-ar Allen going town, me not going drive with you."

It was my first time on a bus. And, when we eventually boarded, a passenger shouted, "Mi-sa-ar Allen, take care you not late for heaven when the time come"

Father responded good-humouredly as Mr Carlton reluctantly stubbed out his cigarette and started the engine.

The bus was crowded. Men were hanging out at the back and there was the occasional cackle from the chickens. I sat in front on father's lap. It was fun. I saw the trees, the telegraph poles and houses moving as the bus drove by. I had never seen them move before so I shouted aloud to the passengers, "Look the trees and the houses are moving."

They were amused; they responded, but I was too excited to hear. Although it was only eighteen miles to the town, the journey was taking forever. At last we arrived in the Market Square.

Mr Carlton called to the passengers as we got off the bus, "We leave at three o'clock"

One of the passengers said to father, "Mi-s-s-a-r, you hear that!"

Father responded, "Go about your business." And holding my hand, he walked across the Market Square.

The town has three main streets – Back, Middle, and Bay. The marketplace straddled all three and formed a square that seemed to divide the town in half. There were no pavements; the streets were wide and busy with people, cars, and buses. I was afraid. There was so much to take in. The houses were large and closer to one another than they are at home in my village. The sea was nowhere to be seen. I stared at everyone and everything. I behaved like a real country bumpkin.

Father held my hand firmly. We crossed the street. I pointed and asked in a loud voice, "Why is that man standing in the middle of the street? Why doesn't he move?"

Father replied, "He is the Iron Man; he is standing there to remind us that he and others like him from St Vincent, fought in a war to save the King in England."

I said, in an even more excitable voice, "But I thought God saved the King."

People I did not know stopped to ask Father about the little one. They talked over my head and then smiled at me as they moved on.

I asked, "Who was that?"

Father replied, "Stop asking so many questions, child. We have to go to Bata's to buy you a pair of shoes, and then I am taking you to stay with your uncle so I can get on with what I came into town to do." Father bought me a pair of shoes at Bata's. They were not white; they did not have any buckles. They were black; they had laces, and they were boys' shoes. I did not like them at all so I cried loudly in the shop and in the street. "I don't like them! I don't like them!"

Father said, "Stop making such a noise, child. Everybody is looking at you. I won't bring you back to town again if you can't behave yourself in the street."

Father arrived at my uncle's at midday. The shops had closed for lunch, and he had not done any of the business he wanted to do. At lunch I overheard him saying that he had brought me into town to buy a pair of shoes for me to wear to school and that I was going to start on the following Monday. It was the first time I was hearing that. My joy and excitement that had begun the day turned to sadness and tears. Nobody had ever asked me if I wanted to go to school. If they had, I would have told them *NO*.

I wept, for I did not want to exchange the freedom I enjoyed with my friends – the stones, the beach, and the sea – for the restriction of the school, where I had no friends. It meant saying a reluctant farewell. It meant wearing boys' shoes, and I did not want to do that. So I cried myself to sleep in my uncle's bed. This was a relief to Father, for he was then free to get on with his business.

We did not get to the Market Square at three o'clock. Instead, Mr Carlton with his passengers stopped at my uncle's home, and as I was still asleep, they waited. As we boarded the bus, a passenger shouted, "L-a-a-r-d- -Mi- s- s- a- r – like father like daughter? Na tell me that she go late for heaven too."

Father smiled and said, "No, not if I can help it." As the years have gone by, I have often wondered what he meant by that remark.

Uplands, is the neighbouring village. It was part of a large colonial estate. A colonial-style house, once the residence of the estate owner, occupied a commanding view and had now become the infant and primary school that children from the three surrounding villages attended.

The road to the school building was up a steep and rugged winding path; at the bottom of the path ran a stream, and older siblings piggybacked the young ones across. Giftey, our young helper, who was new to our family, carried me across. She came to our home with her mother, Mrs Martin, early one Monday morning, carrying a parcel wrapped in newspaper and tied with a string. I saw them from my vantage point on the windowsill as they came into the yard and called out, "Good morning, Ma-a-m."

I had seen them the day before in church, but I did not know their names. They lived in another village and attended the church in Newlands, so I was surprised to see them entering our yard. My mother appeared just as surprised when she replied, "Good morning, Mrs Martin. What can I do for you?"

"Well Ma-a-m, Miss Jackson did tell me after church yesterday that you was looking for a young person to work for you. So me bring me daughter Giftey early before you take on anybody else. We leave home since daybreak to get here before the sun get hot and make the pitch on the road burn she bare foot."

My mother was stunned. But quickly composing herself, she said, "It is true that I spoke to Mrs Jackson yesterday, but I think she may have misunderstood my requirement. I am looking for someone who is older – someone who has already left school. How old is your daughter?"

Mrs Martin turned to her daughter, who had been hiding behind her and said, "Tell Ma-a-m good morning. Tell she your name and how old you be." But her daughter was too shy to speak. Instead, with her eyes glued to the ground and her right foot kicking the sand, she remained silent. So her mother replied, "She name is Giftey. She is ten, going on to eleven years of age. She can wash she own clothes, clean the house, sweep the yard, and wash the wares. She can read, write, and spell she own name. You na have to send she to school every day."

"I am sorry, Mrs Martin, your daughter is too young. I am looking for someone much older."

"Ma-a-m, to tell you the truth, things hard with me and me husband. We got five mouths to feed," and tapping her stomach with her right hand, she added, "with another one on the way. When Miss Jackson tell me that you was looking for somebody for work with you, me did say to myself, this is an answer to prayer. Me know you go look after she and teach she how to do things nice. Me even bring she clothes with me so she can stay with you from now."

At that point my mother saw me on my perch, and realised that I was listening to the conversation. She waved me away from the window and I heard nothing more. Suffice to say, from that day on Giftey became a member of the household. And once she had settled in, she was given the task of taking me to school.

What a chore it was for poor Giftey. Her real name was Elvira. But she was called Giftey because her father had dreamt on the night before her birth that he was going to receive a gift from the Lord. The following day, when the baby was born, he decided that she was the gift that he had been promised in his dream, so the family called her Giftey. The Methodist minister who christened her did not think that it was a suitable name for a child, so he advised the parents to name her Elvira, the same name as her grandmother, who was a staunch member of the church. And they agreed to do so.

Giftey did not enjoy taking me to school. In fact, she dreaded it, for I was not a willing pupil. I cried each morning, rolled on the ground, and made a spectacle of myself. I was quite exhausted by the time I arrived, so I often fell asleep and had to be sent home. On the rare occasions that I remained awake, I sulked, spoke to no one, and made attempts to run away. The teachers said that I was a difficult child.

"She won't go to school." I overheard my mother speaking to my aunt on the telephone. "I don't know what to do with her. I can't leave her with her grandmother. She is not like the others; she does not like to stay there. I can't send her up to you because she would make your life a misery. She is not like the others; she is stubborn and she has a mind of her own. Mark you; the midwife did warn me that she would be like that because she was born with the caul over the face." Babies who were born in this way are said to be blessed with foresight.

My aunt's husband was the headmaster at the school in the village where my grandmother lived. My sister was the head of a primary school. They talked about sending me to one of those schools, but I did not want to go to either of them.

I liked it when Earl, my big brother came home for his holiday because he gave me sweets. He talked to me, he pushed me on his bicycle, and he gave me rides on his back. One day, he told my mother that he would take me to school. I tried to resist but he held my hand firmly, and as we walked along, he made me say good morning to all the old people who were sitting on their doorsteps, and I did not like that.

Mrs Walters, one of the old ladies, usually sat on the front door step with her long flowered skirt tucked between her legs, her greying black hair parted in the middle and braided in four corkscrews. She called out to everyone as they passed by. And this morning she said, "Ayh, Mr Earl? Good morning. I see you taking she to school today."

Earl replied, " Yes. I hear she doesn't like to go to school."

Mrs Walters cackled with delight, "Ah ha! That good for she. She meet she match today."

We walked along the main road. I tugged my hand away and rolled on the ground, crying. Earl gave me a smack, retrieved my hand, and held it even more firmly all the way to the school.

Mr Phillips was the headmaster for the Infants. Earl knew him for they were at school together. They greeted each other, and Earl said, "Arthur, this little sister of mine does not like going to school. She keeps running away, so please keep an eye on her." Arthur agreed and Earl left.

I sat meekly on the little bench while Mr Phillips prepared the classroom. At last the bell rang, and the teachers gathered the children in lines, ready for prayers. I remained seated on the bench. Mr Phillips had forgotten that I was there. The door to the veranda was open; I sneaked out, retraced my steps quickly down the winding path to the stream, crossed it, crossed the main road, and made my way home along the beach, stopping there to play with the stones and boulders. I was happy once more.

I entered the house from the beach entrance and sat on the bench in the dining room swinging my legs. Nobody knew that I was there. My mother was in the store, and Earl had entered the house by that entrance. I heard him telling her, "I had to give her a few smacks. She won't be back. I left her with Arthur. He is keeping an eye on her." They remained in the store talking for some time. Eventually Earl came into the dining room, and he was surprised to see me. He called to my mother, "She is back! Oh my God, she is back!" They both stared at me in disbelief as I continued to swing my legs.

Little did I know that this was to be my last taste of freedom.

They did not send me back to the school at Uplands. I did not have to wear boys' shoes any more and I was happy. Instead, my mother taught me at home to read, to write, and to count. I had my lessons during the mornings after I had waved to the passengers in the buses. I had a slate and pencil, an abacus, and a Royal Reader. One side of the slate was ruled with single lines. The other side was clear.

I liked the abacus because it had pretty beads. I did not like the Royal Reader because the stories were not as good as those in the Anansi books, which were based on the imaginary tales of an Ashanti spider. Anansi was my hero. He played tricks on grown-ups and other animals and always won.

After lunch my mother sent me to bed, and although I spent very little time with my imaginary friends, the rocks, the stones, and the sea, I was happy. Then one day, I overheard Pearl talking to my mother. Pearl asked her, "Did you hear about the Catholic school that is being built next door to the church?"

"No! Does that mean that we would get rid of you know who at last?"

"Yes! I have been asked to be the head of the Juniors. So you see, I would be able to keep an eye on her. There would be no chance of her running away." My heart began to beat rapidly. I knew they were talking about me. And just then, I really wanted to run away.

I had heard that the school in Uplands was due to be closed because it was now too small for the number of pupils. The new two-storied school was built near the mouth of the river and shared its yard with the Catholic Church. Although it was a Roman Catholic school, children of all denominations from the surrounding villages were due to attend.

I had heard that it needed teachers, but that was no concern of mine, for I was being taught very well at home. It was a sad day for me when I overheard that my sister Pearl was going to transfer from her school to become the head of the Juniors of this new school. I knew that with her no-nonsense approach, she was going to take control of my life, my freedom, and my education. Much to my mother's relief and to my great sorrow, I was carted off to the new school a fortnight later.

We had to cross a bridge to get there. The river was wide, with large stones but no sand. Each Monday, women took their clothes to the river to be washed. With their skirts tied between their legs, the women stood in the water. They laughed and exchanged village gossip as they washed and beat the clothes on one of the large stones. It reminded me of the times that I used to flog my imaginary friends at the seashore.

I soon made real friends at the new school. Flora came from another village. She was a Catholic, and she was my best friend. She was allowed to go to catechism every Wednesday afternoon in preparation for her confirmation, so of course I went along with her. I liked the scent of the incense, and the statues of the saints fascinated me. I learnt their names. I learnt to genuflect before the altar, to make the sign of the cross, and to call the priest "Father." These things were new to me, for I was a Methodist, and Methodists did not do those things.

Each Wednesday afternoon we walked in single file from the school, across the schoolyard, to the church. Father Abraham met us at the door. He made the sign of the cross over us. And, leading us to the vestry he asked, "Now, my children – who made you?"

We replied, "God made us."

"And why did God make you, my children?"

"God made us to love him and serve him in this world and the next."

In the vestry we sat on low chairs with faces eager and eyes glued to his as we recited our catechism. The time came when preparation for confirmation was completed and the date was set for First Communion. Father Abraham explained what we were expected to do. It meant nothing to me, but Flora was excited. She told me about her new dress and veil and the preparations that her parents were making. I did not understand what she was talking about; it sounded like preparation for a wedding. So I asked her if she were getting married. She laughed, still full of excitement, and I got caught up in the excitement as well.

My sister, although she was now teaching at the school, did not know that I had been preparing to become a Catholic; neither did my parents, and indeed neither did I. Father Abraham, was Hungarian, and spoke little English. He arrived on his motorbike at our home after church one evening and tried to ask why I had not been to make my first communion; my parents listened to him sympathetically and then tried to explain to him that he had made a mistake. But Father Abraham assured them that he had not. This was quite a revelation for my family, it was the first they were being made aware of my unintended conversion to the Catholic faith.

Poor Father Abraham was lost for words when my parents told him in no uncertain terms that he was wrong to have encouraged me to attend his classes. And, to emphasise her displeasure, my mother stood and in a dismissive tone of voice said, "Father Abraham, we are Methodists. We have no plans to convert to Catholicism at this stage of our lives."

Father Abraham fumbled for words but decided instead to make a hasty retreat. When he left, I overhead my mother saying, "What are we going to do with her? We have only just got her to go to school and now she is preparing to become a Catholic."

Back at school, I was no longer allowed to go to catechism or to visit the church with my friend. My sister saw to that. The only exciting thing about being at school had been taken away from me, and I again longed for the freedom I had enjoyed with my silent friends. And so it was that I had to reluctantly accept that the weekdays were meant for school and the weekends for the family, the rocks, and the stones.

I was always pleased when Saturday came; it meant that I did not have to go to school. Instead, my sister Lena, aged 10, my brother Edward, aged 6, and I, aged 8, went to Dunbar I liked Dunbar. It was the village where my father owned Root Valley, the land he farmed for arrowroot, a yearly produce that was made into starch. Then there was also the cane, for making sugar and rum, as well as other crops, including vegetables and fruits.

In Dunbar, we could eat and drink all the things that we were not allowed to eat and drink at home. Father had the only shop in the village. He was everyone's Godfather and everyone called us Godsister or Godbrother. Godfathers in the village were expected to be benevolent, so the shop did not make a profit.

On the days that we went to Dunbar, we left home after breakfast to avoid the heat of the midday sun. We walked in single file along the main road for one mile before turning inland to walk the further two miles along the narrow, winding, grassy path, passing the Anglican church and cemetery on the way.

Further inland from the church and cemetery was Montana village. Here, the elderly folk would call out to us from their thatched houses or their yards that were cleanly swept. And always with the same refrain: "Marning! How yo' do? All-you going up to Dunbar?"

We would respond politely to each of these greetings, for we knew that if we did otherwise, the carrier pigeons would instantly wing their way back to our home and to Dunbar to complain.

Our journey, although only three miles, took a long time; for it was punctuated by many brief pauses to respond to greetings, followed by further stops to shelter in the shade of the trees from the heat of the sun, and to rest our willing but tired little legs. This did not dampen our spirits; we looked forward to indulging in all the fruits and treats that were awaiting us, and we were never disappointed.

The workers on the land took great delight in egging us on to eat and drink as much we could. The young boys, who were not much bigger than we were, scaled the tall coconuts trees like adept squirrels to shake the fresh coconuts from the trees. They husked them and gave them to us to drink. Then they stood by chuckling as we struggled to balance the coconut and drink the water from the small hole they had pierced. They referred to us as "children from the Bay". They would say to Father, "Them children from the Bay, them not as strong as our children from the land. Them don't know how to climb coconut tree." Father laughingly agreed with them.

Once we were refreshed, we were given our own tasks. We would pick the guavas, collect the nutmegs and breadnuts from under the trees, or shell the green or black-eyed peas. Whatever we collected, and that was never very much, we took home.

Lunch took most of the day to prepare. It was mostly prepared on the land, but occasionally we were treated to Aunt Alice's peas soup. Aunt Alice lived in Dunbar. She was not married, but over the years, she had somehow acquired several nieces and nephews from among the village children. They called her "Tanty", meaning "Auntie". Even those who were perhaps older than her called her Tanty as a mark of respect.

No one made peas soup like Aunt Alice did. All the ingredients came fresh from Root Valley that morning. She cooked her soup in a cast-iron pot, either on an open wood fire or on a coal pot. Usually, one of the neighbour's children would be delegated to fan the fire from time to time to make sure that it did not go out.

By the time lunch was ready and we had eaten it, it was late afternoon and time for us to return home with the produce we had collected. Dusk falls suddenly in the Caribbean, and in the country villages where there were no streetlights, there was very little difference between dusk and total darkness; we were always eager to leave before dusk descended, and father saw to it that we did.

We were particularly anxious to pass the church and cemetery before it became totally dark. In the daytime, although we were inwardly scared when we got to the church, we pretended to be brave. But when it was getting dark it was a different matter, especially as Giftey had told us many stories about jumbies. These were supposed to be special ghosts that came out of the graves at night.

Giftey told us that there were two different types of jumbies. There were the jack-o'-lanterns, which looked like a large ball-like animal that rolled around the road, spitting fire as it did so. Then, there were the acatuses, which were the taller-than-average figures of men, who prevented anyone from passing by standing astride the road. These tales we firmly believed, so when we got to the church and cemetery at dusk we held hands tightly and ran for our lives.

Sunday meant spending the day with my grandmother, going to church, and sitting erect in her pew. Newlands was the village where my grandmother lived and where the nearest Methodist church was located. It was four miles inland from our home. The church service began at eleven o'clock. There were no buses on Sundays, so we left home at seven o' clock to walk the four miles.

The people of Newlands referred to my grandmother as "Mother Reese". Mother Reese was a person of firm principles to whom people went for advice. She was of slender build and wore her grey hair in a tight bun at the back. Her stately bearing had the effect of keeping people at a distance even as they sought her advice. This characteristic came from her childhood experiences. At a young age, she was sent away to school in Barbados and was used to having her own transport in the form of a horse and trap. The villagers referred to her as "the black Miss Harrison" – Harrison being the name of an English estate owner.

My grandmother, we called her "Mama", lived by a set of clearly defined rules. She believed that slippers were only to be worn in the bedchamber, so at home she wore medium-heeled, laced-up shoes with pointed toes and stockings that were rolled in a knot just below the knees. Her dresses were long, made from plain cotton or silk with sleeves that came down to her wrists.

She managed the post office that served the local villages. As the office was located at her home, she adopted a very formal approach in dealing with members of the public. She held firmly to the view that there was "no friendship in business". She preferred not to shake hands with any member of the church who happened to call at the office. There were times when her air of aloofness caused offence to members of the church, and my grandmother was puzzled by their reaction.

The church at Newlands was erected in the centre of the village, on the crest of a hill, and was visible from miles. It had neither a spire nor a clock, so on Sundays, the Sexton rang the bell from the belfry on three occasions, at half-hourly intervals, to remind the villagers of the time and to summon the congregation. We often arrived at our grandmother's one hour before the service began and just as the second peal was ringing.

The members of the congregation came from the surrounding villages of Dunbar, Sharplands, and Lowlands, all within a two-mile radius of unpaved roads and rugged paths. We were the only ones who came from further afield. Everyone wore hats to church and clothes that were set aside specifically for Sundays. Everyone observed the Sabbath. Children did not play outside; we were only allowed to sing hymns, so the village was a very quiet place on Sundays.

The church service was always a sombre and serious event. My grandmother's pew was directly opposite the choir. The minister was not resident in the village, and as there was no opportunity for routine choir practice, the hymns were chosen on the day. Often, there was rivalry between individual members of the choir, who would begin to sing loudly before Mrs Solomon, the organist, had time to strike the first chord. And when the congregation joined in the singing, the discord was further emphasised. Whenever this happened, we giggled, and my grandmother stared disapprovingly at us.

After church we went to her home for lunch and to spend the rest of the day. She lived in a large colonial-style house with a garden that contained fruit trees and sweet-smelling white roses. There was a hammock on the veranda, but there were certain things that were not done on the Sabbath in my grandmother's house, and swinging in the hammock was one of them.

Mama saw herself as responsible for our moral education. Her life was governed by certain strict tenets that she tried to instil in us whenever we visited. We had to sit upright in a chair, and we were forbidden to swing our legs or to fidget. When the grown-ups wanted to speak to one another, we had to leave the room. I found it all very strange and restrictive, but the others seemed not to mind. Embroidered in a frame on her mantelpiece were the words: "As thy days, so shall thy strength be."

She said that we were wild because we lived too near the rough seas. And whenever she found us giggling, she would say, in a stern voice, "There is a time and a place for everything under the heavens," which was always followed by: "Young children should be seen and not heard."

At lunch, there was always freshly made ginger and sorrel beer. But before we could have any of it, each of us had to say our own special grace before meals. This seemed to take a long time, for there were many of us with several graces to be said, and we were by then very hungry. At the end of the meal my grandmother said her own special grace and always ended with the words: "In all thy ways acknowledge him, and he shall direct thy path."

We were never allowed to excuse ourselves from the table. We had to wait to be dismissed. I was always pleased when we were allowed to leave the table, and whilst the others were happy to listen to my grand mother's tales of her youth and to look at old-fashioned pictures and photographs, I hastened to visit her neighbour, Mrs Bolt. Mrs Bolt was a widow who lived in a small cottage at the bottom of my grandmother's garden. And, unlike my grandmother, she was **not** severe.

Mrs Bolt went to the same church as we did. She always carried, in her handbag, a freshly plucked grape leaf, which she used as a fan. She wore various shades of polka-dot dresses and hats with feathers pointing upwards to the sky that matched the colour of the dots. She seemed always pleased to see me and responded to my childish ramblings with an occasional "Oh my" and nodded and smiled encouragingly.

She allowed me to rock in her rocking chair and did not mind that it was the Sabbath. Apart from "Oh my," I cannot recall Mrs Bolt saying anything else. But this did not matter, because she was my friend and I was accustomed to having friends who did not and could not speak.

Chapter 2:
The Village and Its People

In my memory, there were three parts to my village. I suppose it was a sort of trinity. There was that part we called Friendly Village that was wedged between the red cliffs and the seashore and was welcoming to strangers and eccentrics.

Further inland, and across the river there was the estate part of the village that was owned by two colonial brothers who were of Portuguese origin. They provided employment and thatched houses for the workers and their children. Then, there was the pastoral part of the village, comprised of the school, the headmaster, the church, the servers and Father Abraham.

Like the school, the Catholic church served the neighbouring villages. The estate owners from the surrounding estates were of English and Portuguese stock and staunch members. The priests were all of European origin. Father Abraham was not in tune with the culture and lifestyle of the villagers, so he formed a natural alliance with the estate owners who were the church's greatest benefactors.

Each morning, dressed in his white cassock, Father Abraham would roar along the narrow, winding road on his powerful motorbike, acknowledging no one. The villagers, most of whom were not of his faith, would turn their heads as he roared by, raise their chins slightly, and, with a twist of the lip and pointing a thumb over their shoulder, would say, "The white devil gone on his motorbike." And when he returned, they would call out to one another, "The white devil come back."

One evening, Old Macree was sitting in his usual position on a stone in front of his house, puffing away on his chalk pipe. He was known as the village watchman because he kept an eye on everything that was going on and everyone who lived there. Mr Macree called to Harry, his neighbour and said, "Eh eh, Harry, man, me not see de white devil come back on the motorbike this evening. It look like he late today."

The two men walked to the middle of the road, and, using their hands as binoculars, they stared into the distance hoping to see the motorbike and its passenger. But there was no sign of either. No one had seen Old Macree walk further than from his front door to his stone and back, but that evening, armed with a flambeau and a stick, he and his friend Harry walked towards the Bluff, shouting as they went along, "The white devil not come back yet, me a go look for him."

Soon there was a throng of young and not-so-young men being led by Old Macree. He was walking in the middle of the road proclaiming their mission. At the Bluff, they saw the motorbike perched precariously between the rocks below and Father Abraham lying unconscious. Old Macree turned to one of the young men and said with great authority, "You, boy, run and get Nurse Gray. Tell she Father fall off he motor bike and he na-ah breathe. Tell she we a go haul he up to the roadside till she come."

Then with a hue and cry and great commotion, they brought Father Abraham up to the main road for treatment by the nurse.

.Miss Daisy was the local herbalist and masseur. She was a thin, wiry woman, who boasted that her ancestors came from Portugal during the slave trade. She wore her grey-black hair in a long pigtail down the centre of her back and lived with her daughter, Georgina, in a neatly kept thatched house beside the main road. Everyone in the villages called her Miss Daisy out of respect.

An important part of her herbal equipment was an oil tin that she had bought from Miss Frazer, the shopkeeper. With her oil tin, herbs, and bundle of wood she went from village to village in answer to calls for help. And with her ready-made diagnosis of "the belly-peak drop" – the meaning of which was known only to her – she would, on arrival, put together three large stones to steady the oil tin, fill it with water, Canadian healing oil, and herbs from her garden. Then, undoing her bundle of wood, she would place it between the stones under the oil tin, strike a match and wait for her infusion to boil. From under her long pinafore, she would pull out her chalk pipe and smoke – giving the impression that all was under her control.

Miss Daisy had been sweeping her yard with the broom that she had made from the branches of the coconut tree when Father Abraham roared by on his motorbike. She had made the sign of the cross and genuflected. She had seen him "turn the corner at the Bluff" as the roaring of his machine died away

The noise of Father Abraham's machine had faded away when "Matty, her neighbour's daughter passed by with a bucket of water on her head. She called out, "Aye, Miss Daisy, you hear wha happen to Father Abraham?

"Father Abraham?" she asked. "He just roar pass here as good as gold. Wha happen to he?"

"The motorbike throw he over the Bluff. Them think he dead."

"He can't dead! Me make the sign of the cross when he pass by just now."

"Well Mr Macree and them boys and de nurse just pull he and the bike off the rock below the Bluff."

"Oh!" said Miss Daisy. "Ah, that what make the noise from the bike stop so sudden. Me going to see what me can do for help nurse with him."

With that she scurried off to her back garden, picked some of her herbs, gathered up a bundle of wood from under her house, and placed the herbs in the oil tin she carried under her arm. She changed her head tie and pinafore and hurried off in the direction of the Bluff.

The commotion led by Mr Macree was in full blast. Father Abraham was now lying on the side of the road. Nurse Gray was trying to render first aid whilst the numbers of onlookers were increasing at a steady pace. Suddenly a voice said, "All of you move out of me way." And Miss Daisy elbowed her way through the onlookers. Then, falling on her knees beside Nurse Gray, she said, "Nurse, me come for help you. Thank God he not dead yet." And with those words, she produced a bottle of smelling salts and dangled it under Father Abraham's nostrils.

He shifted and coughed. "Good!" she said, "You see he life coming back."

Poor Father Abraham was at the mercy of Miss Daisy, who was now giving instructions to those around her. "Send for Mr Arthur truck for take Father to the vestry. Me will go ahead for get the oil tin on the fire so me go ready for 'noint him when he reach."

Nurse Gray seemed suddenly to awake from a dream and said with great authority, "No, Miss Daisy, you cannot 'noint Father. No woman is allowed to undress a priest. The church doctrine says that only the Pope can disrobe a priest." And turning to the onlookers, she said, "Will you all please leave now?"

The crowd suddenly backed away. Some made the sign of the cross, whilst others genuflected.

Mr Macree and his friend Harry, feeling that the order to leave did not apply to them, turned and waved the crowd away saying, "All you hear what Nus say? She say go home, all a you. She not want you here. You can't do nothing for Father now."

Miss Daisy rose to her feet and said as she bowed, "Father, forgive me. Me not did mean to disrespect you. Me go come to confession on Saturday evening." Then, making the sign of the cross, she gathered her bundle and hurried home, saying the Hail Mary as she did so.

Nurse Gray was once more in control, and turning to Mr Macree and Harry, who were still hovering in the background, she said, "You too, Mr Macree. And you too, Harry You have done your bit to help Father. You go away and leave Father and his dignity to me."

Mr Macree shook his head as he rose to his feet muttering the word "dignity" as he did so. He turned and looked at Harry with a puzzled expression, and asked, "Harry, man, you did see Father with any dignity when we did take he and de motorbike off the rock? What is this dignity Nurse talking about?"

They were still walking towards their home, wearing the puzzled expression, when Mr Arthur's van passed by, carrying Father Abraham and Nurse Gray over the bridge and back to the vestry. Mr Macree stopped briefly and, placing his hands on his hips, said to the wind, the cliffs, and the sea, "You pass us now. If we not been come out to look fo you, you would of been dead by now." Then, quickening his pace to catch up with Harry, the two men strode on, each in deep thought.

The pastoral part of the village included the Catholic church and school. The land for the church to be built on had been given by the estate owners. Later, the school was erected and although it was known as the Roman Catholic School, the Colonial Government was responsible for its funding. This meant that the influence of the church was limited.

Each morning we said our Catholic prayers and genuflected. The headmaster, known by everyone as Teacher Sampson, was not a Catholic. But he used his tact and diplomacy to develop a harmonious relationship with Father Abraham and to foster a greater understanding between the church and the people. So it was that both church and school were able to welcome strangers and to promote ethical and moral living in the village.

Teacher Sampson formed links with the village elders, and at the end of each year – usually on the last Friday of the term – he would invite the local group to dance the Quadrille - (a traditional Creole dance.

On those occasions we sat cross-legged on the floor, enthralled as these sprightly elderly women, barefooted but elegantly dressed in long white skirts with brightly coloured sashes and matching head ties, danced to the music of the local banjo and shack-shack band.

These combined aspects of village life brought a special dynamism to the community. We tolerated and accepted a certain degree of eccentric behaviour and the acts of gentle madness displayed by many of the permanent and transient members. We lived in a formal but friendly co-existence with one another. Grown-ups were referred to as Mr and Miss even after the women were married. The age at which you became a grown-up was fluid, but somehow everyone seemed to agree on a time.

Monique – that's what we called her – was one of the non-permanent members of the community. She was a tall, elegant black woman, who was a native of the French West Indian island of Martinique. She appeared in the village one day and decided to stay.

Her style of dress was French Creole. During the week she wore brightly coloured long skirts tucked in a ruffle at the side and a matching head tie, so stiffly starched that it stood erect on her head and added to her upright bearing and elegance. On Sundays, her gown and head tie were sparklingly white. Monique spoke to no one but herself, walked in the middle of the road, ignored the traffic, and lived to die from natural causes.

At first Monique's presence in the village aroused much curiosity. It was rumoured that she had been jilted at the altar in her homeland, and the shock of being jilted in that way made her lose her ability to speak. One of the teachers said that she was like Miss Haversham – a Dickens character. The children, who had never heard of Dickens or of Miss Haversham, nicknamed her "Haf a Ham", and whenever they saw her, they would surround her and chant "Haf a Ham, Haf a Ham." Whenever this happened, Monique would further extend her elegant neck, gaining a few inches as she did so, and without changing her pace or displaying any sign of annoyance, continue to walk in the middle of the road, muttering to herself as if nothing was happening around her. Monique would walk into the shops, stand erect, and wait for the shopkeeper to acknowledge her presence. She would then point at what she wanted to buy. The shopkeepers knew that she always bought in half portions and she would indicate her requirements with gestures. The children who followed her into the shops were convinced more than ever that she was indeed Miss Haf a Ham.

Then suddenly one day, Monique was nowhere to be seen. No one knew when she left or where she went. We searched for her in the neighbouring villages without success. Later we learnt that she was admitted to an institution. And whenever people from the village paid her a visit, although she never spoke, they knew from the sudden sparkle in her eyes that she was pleased they had not forgotten her.

Norm, for that was what every one called him, was a minstrel. Except for the 20-year-old blind son of Mr Shankley, Norm spoke to no one; nor did he accept any charity. He played the flute, led the hearse at funerals as an uninvited guest, and left when the service was over. No one knew where he came from or where he lived, but everyone knew that when Norm arrived in the village there was going to be a funeral. We would awake early in the morning to the sound of his flute, and we knew that someone would die and be buried by the end of the day. It was uncanny but true.

At first the community was wary of his presence, but when Norm began to teach Mr Shankley's blind son to play the flute, the villagers warmed towards him. Until that time, "Blind Shankley", for that was what everyone called him, was a recluse, who lived with his elderly father and was occasionally seen sitting on his front door step blowing into a flute. Norm not only taught him how to play the flute, but he also became his eyes, and together they travelled around the villages as minstrels. Now we had both Norm and Blind Shankley as uninvited guests leading the funeral cortege.

But unlike Blind Shankley, Norm travelled further afield, as if guided by a sixth sense. Shankley remained in nearby villages. Then one day someone died and Norm was not there. We knew something was wrong. We never saw him again, and no one knew what had happened to him. But he had left us with a minstrel, a minstrel who would have liked to have led the cortege of his only friend.

The village also had its entrepreneurs and small businesses. There were bakers – three altogether. Two dressmakers – Miss Yates, a recluse with a selective clientele, and Miss Brown, who was less selective – provided a service for most of the women who lived on the estate.

Then there was Mr Fisher, the shoemaker. His shoe repair business was more of a hobby than a business as most of the villagers walked barefooted. He lived with his wife and grown-up children in a two-storied stone-built house that was painted white. The shoe repair business occupied the ground floor, which had its entrance to the main road. Mr Fisher had fought in the First World War and had lost a leg. He had what the people in the village called a "Cork Leg" and occasionally, when he needed to repair the shoe that was attached to it, he would hang the shoeless cork leg on the wall in his shop.

Mr Fisher took an interest in the spiritual well-being of the children in the village, for apart from the Catholic Church, there was no other church within easy walking distance. So each Sunday at ten o'clock, he held a Sunday school in his yard and invited the children who did not normally attend church. They sat on benches and stones and listened whilst he read them Bible stories. His wife played the piano, and the children sang hymns loudly and out of tune. Mr Fisher's Sunday school was very popular with the children, for they were usually rewarded with a drink and homemade cake at the end.

No one knew how our dog, Fido, discovered Mr Fisher's Sunday school arrangement, but he also became a regular attendee and was never late. The villagers were intrigued by this; he would stand at the bottom of the stairs, waiting for the first chord to be struck. Then he would go bounding up the steps to sit quietly amongst the children. When we learnt of Fido's interest in religion, we decided to rename him, and his name was officially changed from Fido to "Sunday School".

There was a mixed reaction to this name. Florence King, we called her "Flo", was a "born-again Christian". She was particularly perturbed. We overheard her muttering that dogs should not be called Sunday school, as they can't go to heaven.

She was a tall, slender black woman, with an upright, almost regal bearing – the kind of bearing that would have been associated with debutants of a bygone age. But she was not a debutant. Her regal stature was cultivated from years of carrying baskets of vegetables and fruits on her head. She had only one arm, she lived in Dunbar, and worked for my father in Root Valley.

Flo did not work on Sundays. On the other days she walked the three miles from Root Valley to our home with a basket on her head. She did this regardless of the weather and always arrived before we had started preparing our breakfast. The basket contained fresh fruits, vegetables, meat, and milk.

In Root Valley, Father kept his own livestock – pigs, cows, goats, chickens, and turkeys. I cannot remember seeing any sheep during my early years. As the pigs produced their piglets, each of us was given one and told that we were to look after it. We rarely did.

We got our milk mainly from the cows but occasionally from the goats. We always boiled it and made our own butter from the cream on the top of the milk. We also made our own bread, which went well with our homemade butter. Flo liked my mother's bread, but she was not keen on our butter, though she was too polite to say so. Her excuse was always the same: "Butter make me sweat, and when me sweat, me catch a cold."

She was reserved. We were never told; nor were we allowed to ask how she had lost her arm; she was not the kind of person who gave information readily. She responded to questions mostly in monosyllables and never volunteered more than she felt was necessary. Her home was a small thatched house that she shared with her three boys.

We were fond of Flo, and, in a peculiar sort of way, I think that she was fond of us too. She knew that we were always happy to see her, and she knew that it was not because of what she brought. She was a source of fascination and amazement to us. From the upstairs landing, we looked out for her each morning as she turned the corner at the Bluff, with the basket poised firmly on her cotta, a cloth pad that we believed cushioned the discomfort of carrying the basket. Flo always refused any offer of assistance with the unloading of her basket. She never spilt or damaged any of the contents. We did not understand how she was able to lift her basket with its contents with such ease.

Whenever Flo was asked about her three sons, her answer was always the same: "They are well, thank you, Ma-am." When asked how they were getting on at school, she responded, "They are doing well, thank you, Ma-am." The boys were not doing as well as Flo thought. But how was she to know? For she left her home before they went off to school and returned home after school had ended.

There were no schools in Dunbar, so her boys attended one in the neighbouring village of Newlands. The school was two miles away along rugged roads and winding paths. The children from Dunbar did not find the temptation to be truant difficult to resist, and Flo's boys were no exception.

Secrecy and privacy were not part of the culture of the people who lived in Dunbar. So my father soon learnt of the boys' escapades. Without seeking Flo's permission, Father took control of the situation. He arranged for the boys to be followed and to be apprehended. He organised their transfer to the school in the village, where my sister was now teaching. Flo was told that in future her boys would go with her to the village each morning and would attend the school there. She did not object to the interference in her domestic arrangements, for my father was godfather to all the children in the village, and as far as the parents were concerned, he knew what was best for them. In the case of Flo's boys, this turned out to be true. The three of them have had successful careers and have made a significant contribution to the community.

Mr Banks had his own church in his home village of Roland Park. It was what the islanders referred to as a "clap hand, tie head church" (Evangelical). Apart from the immediate male members of his family, his followers were women. They wore long, sparklingly white and stiffly starched gowns with wide sky-blue waistbands and head ties to match. They tithed, sang lustily and often out of tune, clapped their hands, shook their tambourines, caught the Spirit, spoke in tongues, and fell prostrate on the floor. In the late 1940s and early 1950s, Mr Banks was the only baker in the village of Roland Park and the women bought their bread from him. He used this daily contact to spread the gospel of his church to them. In our village, we had heard of Mr Banks as the good Christian man who was spreading God's words through his flourishing church.

Doris Duncan, Eileen Lewis, and Lucita Milligan were the bakers in our village. Together they provided bread and cakes for the four nearby villages. They baked their bread in specially built clay ovens that were housed in a separate building beside their kitchens. We had our own smaller version, for family use only. Doris Duncan lived across the road from us. As children, we used to stand on the window seat and try to count the number of trays that she brought out of her oven.

Doris baked her bread as usual one Saturday. It was a double load, for no baking was ever done on the Sabbath. She packed the wooden trays and covered them with towels made from bleached flour bags. She placed them on the heads of her two daughters and sent them off to the neighbouring villages to sell. By four o'clock, with the baking and selling done as dusk fell, the family and village settled down to rest. It must have been about nine o'clock. It was very dark outside, but the gas lamp in the drawing room was still burning brightly, for my sister Pearl was marking her pupils' books. Suddenly there was a loud bang on the door. Mrs Jenkins stood on the landing, dishevelled and bloodstained.

My sister was surprised to see her and asked, "Mrs Jenkins! What's wrong?"

"Miss Pearl me beg you please call de ambulance. Doris deh pan dead."

"What?" said my sister as she grabbed the key to unlock the downstairs door.

"Doris been in labour all day. Me been telling she for stop de baking but she won't listen. Now the baby born dead. The afterbirth won't come out and she bleeding. Me can't stop it. Nurse Gray gone to Roland Park for deliver twins. Only the ambulance can help Doris now."

The telephone system was old fashioned and temperamental. My sister dialled the exchange and said, "Please connect me to the Colonial Hospital in Kingstown. We need an ambulance urgently for a woman living in our village."

The voice from the end of the line said, "I am sorry, but the lines to Kingstown are down. They have been down all day, and the linesmen won't be working on them again until Monday. I cannot put you through."

Mrs Jenkins placed her hands on her head, screamed loudly, and fell to the floor.

"Come on, Mrs Jenkins let us put our heads together and think. Let us send one of the men to ask Mr Arthur to lend us his truck to take Doris to the clinic in Cedars. At least if we get her to Cedars, where there is a doctor, he would be able to do something."

Just then, there was another knock on the door. This time it was Mr Duncan. He said, "Don't bother call the ambulance; she just breathe she last. She dead." The villagers were shocked for they had bought bread and cakes from her earlier in the day. They were unaware that she was in labour. Doris and her family were well liked and respected. There were seven children of school age and under and a husband who worked on the land and knew nothing about the bakery.

Mr Duncan was in a quandary. At first the villagers rallied around and offered support. Later, relatives came from the neighbouring islands of Grenada, Trinidad, and Barbados. They offered to take some of the children to live with them. Whether dazed from the shock of his wife's sudden death or recognising that he would not be able to cope, Mr Duncan agreed that the three girls should go to these relatives. So it was that Mary went to live with an aunt in Trinidad, Gloria to an aunt in Grenada, and Sarah to an Aunt in Barbados. We never saw them again.

Now the village was short of a baker and the boys who were left were too young to carry on the tradition. To the rescue came Mr Banks. He offered to take over the Duncans' bakery, and would have done so had not the other bakers objected. Mrs Milligan said, "Me not trust that man. He eyes too long. I hear that he does carry on with the women in his church. We not want somebody like that in our village."

Mrs Lewis, who had six daughters, said, ""Eh hey, me agree with you. All a we na want he here."

So the Lewises and the Milligans did a deal with Mr Duncan. They rented his oven and sent Mr Banks back to his home and church in Roland Park.

The main form of employment and biggest employer was the estate. Being employed by and also living on the colonial master's estate meant that the workers had less freedom and very little money. In some ways not only were the grown-ups in bonded employment, but so were their children. Women worked long hours.

The estate owner was responsible for providing the workers with their means of relaxation. On The village pasture a plot of land was made into a cricket pitch for his workers. This was next door to the Catholic church and school. Inter-village cricket matches were played there. On those occasions young women known as "club ladies", each dressed in white and each carrying a tin of talcum powder, would sit in the thatched tent that was erected for the purpose. Older men with their banjos would also arrive at the tent, and whenever a cricketer was bowled out, one of the club ladies, accompanied by a banjo player, would escort the cricketer off the field, showering him with her talcum powder.

Most Fridays, somewhat reluctantly but out of the necessity to increase their weekly output for their bosses, parents accepted the unwritten rule that their children would be called upon to work in the fields. The smaller children, usually girls, were sent to collect the arrowroot in heaps, whilst the bigger ones who were mainly boys, were sent to guide the bullock-drawn carts that carried the arrowroot from the field to the factory; others were sent to dig the peanuts. And all of this was done without complaint in the heat of the sun.

The headmaster, Teacher Sampson, felt that the education of the children was too important a matter to be ignored. So on Mondays when the children returned to school, they were punished. This action led to tension between the headmaster, the parents, and the children. And when the estate owners attempted to intervene, the headmaster rose to the challenge, defended his action, and called upon the Father Abraham, his assistants, and the nuns for support.

Father Abraham found himself in a dilemma. He was caught between the church's need to adopt a moral and ethical stance and the desire to maintain its relationship with the estate owners, who were amongst its wealthy benefactors. In the end the church lent its support to the headmaster and persuaded the estate owners to do likewise. So it was that in the intervening years the three parts of the village formed a trinity of a contented and hard working community that lived in peaceful coexistence.

But change was in the offing. Shell's Oil Refineries in the Dutch Antillean islands of Aruba and Curacao needed workers. The advertisement attracted men from the English-speaking Caribbean islands. Men who in the past had worked on the estate now had a choice and the opportunity to earn more money, to improve their standard of living, and to educate their children. As the years went by and the younger generation became more educated, there was a shortage of local labour available to the estate owners. One by one the large estates were divided into plots of land and sold. Those people who once were labourers on the estates were now able to buy the land, to build houses, and to become farmers themselves. Today, on the plot of land that overlooked the cricket pitch, where the club ladies cheered the local cricketers, stands a resource centre that provides further educational opportunities for the wider community.

"Things happen in threes." That was a common expression on the island. The significance of this became a reality for me whilst I was in my first year at high school. I felt that my world had taken a summersault. In fact, there were several summersaults during that period, and I began to wonder whether the turbulence would ever cease.

The first experience of turbulence came when I left my friends at the Catholic school in the village to start a new life as a pupil at the Girls' High Shool in Kingstown and to become a Boarder. Moving to Kingstown was to have been the beginning of a life of order and regimentation. And yet for me, it was an unsettling time as it separated me from the tranquillity of, the sea, and the timelessness.of the countryside where I had always cherished that feeling of time as being a languid affair..

At the new school, there were uniforms to be worn, timetables to be kept, and different teachers and subjects to accommodate. How I missed the peace that I had left behind. And as if that were not enough for a reluctant pupil to contend with, my sister Pearl became my form mistress. I felt a sense of foreboding descending on me throughout this period of disruption.

I did not know what form and shape this premonition would take. I just felt nervous that events were developing beyond my control. I looked forward to the end of term when I could return home to my village to be free once more. But that was not to be, for I had not been home a week when news came from Newlands that my grandfather was unwell. He had recently returned home to retire after eighteen years of working abroad. For this reason he had not played as active a part in the church and in shaping the lives of his grandchildren as my grandmother had.done.

The news held no significance for me. Everyone I knew had always made a full and speedy recovery whenever they were ill. This was not to be so where my grandfather was concerned. He died within a few days. It was my first experience of dealing with a death in the family. It was all quite unreal. There was the church service, the coffin, the wreaths, the grown-ups dressed in black, the tears being shed, and bewildered children dressed in black and white.

His was a simple service in keeping with his wishes. Then there was a sudden panic as the wreaths were being laid, for it was discovered that one was missing. That was considered to be a bad omen. It meant that another member of the family would soon be following him on that journey to heaven.

I felt that I needed to look over my shoulder constantly to make sure that I was not the one that Mr Death was coming to take with him. I stayed close to home, became very quiet and compliant, and did all the right things. In fact, I had become so saint-like that my family thought I was ill.

It was my grandmother who, six months later, followed her husband. The funeral routine by this time was familiar to me, although the service lasted longer as the ministers and stewards paid their separate tributes to the person they referred to as "one of God's true disciples". Later, when the wreaths were being laid, we made sure that none was left behind.

What was happening to my world? There would no more Sundays in Newlands, no more singing out of tune in the church, and saddest of all, there would be no more visits to my friend Mrs Bolt, who indulged me in my childish ramblings, allowed me to rock in her rocking chair on the Sabbath, and encouraged me with her gentle "Oh my".

Now that the mystery of who was to follow my grandfather had been solved, I breathed a sigh of relief. I felt that I'd had a lucky escape and I began to relax once more. School and boarding in the capital continued to be something I endured rather than enjoyed. I made very few friends; in fact I was referred to as "the quiet one". That suited me very well, for it meant that no one expected me to engage in polite conversation and I could be left alone with my thoughts and my daydreaming, and for that I was grateful.

Someone somewhere seemed to have made a decision that peace and tranquillity were no longer to become a significant part of my life. School closed for the Christmas holiday and as usual, I was delighted to be going home. There was always a great deal of preparation for the season. At the beginning of Advent, we organised a family concert at home and invited neighbours. We made up our own plays and performed to our audience. My mother baked special cakes for the occasion.

By Christmas week, the festivities had taken hold. All the members of the family had returned home. Father was winding down his activities in Dunbar and had made sure that the employees had all that they needed. His shop was thriving from the sale of goods for which very few customers paid. We expected him to come home early on Christmas Eve, but when dusk descended and he had not arrived, we set out to meet him as a surprise. We passed Montana village and were now on the last leg towards Dunbar. There were no houses, only a few mango trees and cane and arrowroot fields along this stretch of the road.

As we walked we saw someone leaning against a tree. We thought that someone had started his celebration early and collapsed in a drunken stupor. But it was not a drunk; it was our father, who was having a heart attack.

Father did not die on Christmas Eve, but the family celebrations were cancelled. In times of crisis, grown-ups have a tendency to make decisions without involving the young.

I knew that Father was ill because he was rushed to the hospital in Kingstown. Yet I was told nothing. I knew that something was gravely wrong, for the grown-ups spoke in hushed voices and stopped whenever I approached. Their anxiety consumed me. I no longer spent time at the seashore. Instead, I spoke in whispers and tiptoed around the house.

My harmonious relationship with the sea, the rocks, and the stones changed. I became insecure, tense, and full of gloom. The mountainous waves that splashed against the huge black rocks suddenly became a menacing herald of doom. This feeling of doom disturbed my peace of mind and made me apprehensive and fearful. I felt the need to stay close to home and to seek protection from the clouds that were gathering around in readiness to overwhelm me.

This was the atmosphere I lived in throughout the Christmas holiday until mid-January, when I returned to school. But there too I felt distracted and preoccupied. When I visited Father in the hospital, he was breathing through a mask and spoke in gasps. Nurses stood around with sympathetic expressions and shook their heads knowingly. I wanted to ask if he was going to die. But I felt that there was no one who was willing to answer that question.

Early in the morning on 20 January, I was told that I would not be going to school that day, for Father had died in the early hours of the morning and was to be buried that evening. I felt numb and once more overcome with anxiety and fear.

Funerals in the West Indies are not a private family affair. The early-morning radio programme carries the death announcements. It is the easiest means of informing relatives and friends. I did not hear the announcement that day, but there must have been one, for busloads of people dressed in black came from the country villages.

Mrs Trent, a middle-aged woman, heard the announcement and, unable to afford the fare, walked for most of the eighteen miles from our village and arrived on time. My brother Earl was not so fortunate, for he lived and worked abroad. His journey had started two days earlier, but on arrival in Trinidad he was informed that his onward flight to our island had been cancelled. In desperation, he travelled by boat, but the boat developed engine trouble and had to dock in Grenada. The delay meant that he missed the opportunity for him to say goodbye to his father

In most of the islands during the 1950s, there were certain protocols and norms to be followed whenever a member of the family died. There was a specified period for mourning, mode of dress, and behaviour to be observed. On the day of the funeral I was presented with a black and white dress for the occasion. And for the first three months following Father's death, I wore black and white dresses; for the following three months I wore grey, and the next three I wore white. And during that period, as a mark of respect, no member of the family attended any celebration.

The family rented a bungalow by the sea for a fortnight so that we could spend time together undisturbed, to discuss and to make plans for the future. There were six children still to be educated. There was no one available to take over the reins in Root Valley or to manage the shop.

It was Father's wish that the land should remain in the family. I worried about the school fees, about my pocket change, and about leaving our home in the village. I was relieved when it was decided that we would build a home in the Capital and, retain the house in the village and the land at Root Valley. I think I smiled for the first time that year.

We rented a house in the centre of the town whilst our new home was being built. We were delighted that we no longer needed to be boarders. The new house was built on a hill that overlooked the town and harbour. From its porch we were able to enjoy magnificent views of the sea, the Grenadines, and amazing sunrises and sunsets.

Father's death was a turning point for me. He was the provider for the family. I knew that I would never again be able to say, "*Father, I want...*". So I curbed my free spirit and settled down at school. I learnt to be responsible, to take care of my possessions, and not to make unnecessary demands. In fact I think I grew up; I developed a different perspective on life and learnt to value all that I once had taken for granted.

Home - Not Native Land

Yesterday I stood at the window
That overlooked the sea.
The sea became an ocean,
An ocean wide and deep.

I felt the urge to wander
Far beyond
The great expanse of water
To a distant land.

I had no thought of where
Or why I needed to
Explore an unknown country
And leave my native land.

But yet I did,
And here I am in England,
A country I call home –
Not native land.

Chapter 3:
Leaving Home

The year was 1957. I had just been given my first job. I say given, for I had not applied nor had I a burning desire to work in an office. I was resisting the family, who wanted me to go to the University of the West Indies in Jamaica to undertake a Diploma in Education. But I wanted to attend the theological college to become a Methodist deaconess.

"You are too young to become a deaconess in the Methodist church, so do not argue with us. We know what is best for you. We know that you mean well. But we have asked our Superintendent Minister and our Deaconess Sister Margaret. They both agree with us that you are far too young to be shouldered with that kind of responsibility." Those were the final words spoken by the family on the subject, and I accepted defeat.

It was also at this time that my brother-in-law and the Warden of the Town Board conspired together to offer me a post at the Board. All I needed to do on that Saturday afternoon was to accompany my brother-in-law to the Town Board office to be introduced to the Warden. The post would be mine and I would commence working on the following Monday.

As I walked into the office on that Saturday afternoon, I saw a number of girls whom I knew. They were sitting in an anteroom. It did not occur to me until many months later that they were waiting to be interviewed for the post that I had been given and for which I did not apply.

Nepotism was a norm in St Vincent, so it was never challenged. And, although I knew that I did not have the secretarial skills that some of the other interviewees had, I did not question the manner in which I was appointed In later years, I have reflected with some discomfort on the way in which nepotism was interwoven within the structure of the society, and I have endeavoured not to practice it in my working life.

The Town Board's office was a prefabricated building located in the poor area of Kingstown, tucked away from the main Civil Service buildings and offices. There was, however, one redeeming factor; our salary scales were higher than those of the civil servants. Apart from the Accounts Clerk and me, all other employees were male. There were no female members of the Board. We dealt with market traders, road sweepers, plumbers, gravediggers, and refuse collectors, all of whom were male. Most of them came to the office bringing tales of rich life experiences with the singular intention of embarrassing the two young girls, whom they felt had no right to be working in a man's world.

In the 1950s, the United Kingdom was actively recruiting young men and women from the larger Caribbean Islands to train as nurses for the newly established National Health Service (NHS). There was no active recruitment in St Vincent. However, it became routine for Italian liners to weigh anchor in to the harbour on Sunday afternoons to take on board enthusiastic young people who were fired with ambition, excitement, and anticipation of entering a noble profession in the Mother Country. They dreamt of seeing the sites they had read about, of experiencing the history that they had been taught, and of discovering the beauty of the countryside. They hoped to see the fair daffodils and the Old Vicarage Granchester, with its church clock stuck at ten to three, and have honey for tea in "England's green and pleasant land".

On those Sunday afternoons, the harbour was full of young people saying goodbye to friends and parents with lumps in their throats and tears in their eyes. Young lovers stole that last kiss, as they wept and made promises to each other whilst the liner piped out the sentimental tune "I Saw Those Harbour Lights",

Little did they know how soon their worthy aspirations would be depleted by their experiences. And like the fair daffodils, they would see their good intentions waste away into a state of disappointment, disillusionment, and depression from which recovery would be difficult and the scars would remain.

I had no plans to join the young adventurers. I wanted to remain in the West Indies The teaching profession and the Civil Service were not fields I wished to explore. So it was that I began secretly to submit applications to hospitals in England.

I did not share this course of action with the rest of the family until I had received a letter of acceptance from a hospital called Rush Green in the county of Essex. I liked the sound of it. I pictured it as part of the rich tapestry that went to make up the green and pleasant land of England. Once more, the family took control of the situation and made enquiries of our resident Methodist Deaconess who came from Malden in Essex. She was asked to find out whether the hospital was an acceptable one.

In life, history has a way of repeating itself. Like the previous arrangement that was made between my brother-in-law and the Warden, the family, the Methodist Deaconess, the British Council, and the Matron of Essex County Hospital arranged for me to undertake my training at the Essex County Hospital in Colchester. My family were happy with the new arrangement, and I left home one sunny day in March 1958 and travelled to Trinidad, where I boarded the French Liner the SS *Antilles*, bound for England.

I had a single cabin for the journey. Once on board, the Steward took charge of my suitcases and showed me to my cabin. Noticing that the door could not be locked, I drew this to his attention. He apologised and promised to return to fix it. When he did not, I mentioned it to two female passengers from Guyana, who were travelling together. They exchanged strange glances and spoke sternly and in unison.

"He said he is coming back to fix it? Did he? Where is your cabin? You are travelling with us. We have a four-berth." With that they collected my suitcases, and they installed me in their cabin, where I stayed for the entire journey. It was many months later that I understood the significance of their action.

The journey took fourteen days. For the first five, we docked in various islands, where other passengers joined us. This aspect of the voyage was exciting. We spent the day ashore, and we sailed at night. Our last port of call was St Kitts and when we departed, we saw no land for the following nine days. The ocean was calm; from the deck it looked like an aquamarine carpet stretching to the horizon.

As the days went by, I became anxious and homesick. Reality was dawning, albeit somewhat belatedly. I realised that I was on my own; I had no relatives to turn to, and I was going to a strange land to undertake training for a profession I had chosen in a pique of rebellion against my family.

The SS *Antilles* weighed anchor in Plymouth Harbour early one Sunday morning in March. The passengers, all smartly but some inappropriately dressed for the climate, queued for passport scrutiny and then disembarked to board the boat train for London. I was alone and apprehensive. I stood on the deck for what to me seemed an eternity, until a prim middle-aged woman with a matter-of-fact manner approached. "Are you for British Council?"

Relieved, I replied, "Yes, I am."

"Do you know the drill?"

"No, I don't."

"Well then listen carefully. This green tag that I am going to pin on your coat will identify you as a British Council student. One of my colleagues will be at the station in London to meet you. Come along now and let me settle you on the train for Paddington. We don't have much time. Are these your suitcases?"

"Yes, they are."

"You will need help with them."

And with those words, she descended the gangway, leaving me standing and staring hopelessly at the disappearing figure. She returned, followed by a young man who took charge of the cases, and off we went in single file to the train, where I was settled. With a curt goodbye, she did another disappearing act and vanished in the crowd. Now I was left alone to wrestle with the anxiety of knowing that the green tag matched my coat, and I feared that her colleague would not be able to identify me when I got to Paddington.

This was my first train journey, and it was taking forever. The other passengers were chatting excitedly. Relatives and friends were meeting them. For the first time since leaving home, I felt despair. There was a lump in my throat, an empty feeling in my stomach, and my mouth was dry. I not only felt alone but I knew that I was alone and lonely, even on the crowded train with fellow passengers from the West Indies. Although it was March and springtime, there were no daffodils and no flowers to be seen. The countryside was dark and depressing. The houses all seemed to be attached to one another, and there was smoke coming out of the chimneys. It was so dreary that I wished I had not left my warm and comfortable home, but it was too late to turn back. I wanted to cry but was too embarrassed to do so. My vision of England as that green and pleasant land faded further as the journey progressed, and I wondered how I would survive.

It was dark when we arrived in Paddington. There was the buzz of an eager crowd waiting to welcome the new arrivals. I recognised no one. My eyes searched for the British Council representative in vain. Strange men asked me if I were being met and I assured them that I was. Gradually the crowd dispersed. With eyes still searching, I said a silent prayer, and then at last someone tapped me on the shoulder. It was the British Council representative. "We have been looking for you everywhere. Where are you going?"

"To Colchester," I replied

"Oh dear!" she said, looking at her watch. "We haven't got much time, for the last train to Colchester leaves at 9.18 p.m." With those words, and in a fog of utter bewilderment, I was hurried to the car and we sped across London to a station she called Liverpool Street.

We made it with a few minutes to spare, and I caught the 9.18 train to Colchester. The British Council representative exchanged words with the train driver, assured me that I would be met at the station, and then waved me a smiling goodbye. She must have heaved a sigh of relief. But for me, it was an inhalation of even greater apprehension, tempered by the excitement that I was at last about to meet friendly faces that would be warmly welcoming, as implied in the recruitment literature.

It was an unnerving experience to be surrounded by darkness and to be seated alone in the compartment of a moving train, shivering, not from the cold, but from something that I could not define. I hoped that the train driver would remember to stop at Colchester. He did. But there was no one to meet me as promised. So the Stationmaster took control of the situation, for it was almost midnight. He hailed a taxi and said, "This young lady is for the County."

"Not the County, I am going to Essex County Hospital. They are expecting me."

"I know, Ducky," replied the taxi driver as he drove away into the darkness.

We arrived at the nurses' home. The high iron gates were locked and chained. There was a dim light in one of the rooms on the upper floor. We rang the bell and rattled the chain, but there was no response. We continued in our efforts and were eventually rewarded by the spectacle of a figure dressed in a long white robe, wearing a night cap over a pigtail, and who, in a tone as frosty as the night said, "Nurse, you know that you should not come to the front entrance of the nurses' home after 9.00 p.m. You should have gone to Night Sister's office in the main hospital, and she would have let you in."

I do not recall my response to the greeting and being called "nurse", but I know that I was ushered into the lobby of the dimly lit nurses' home, where I was told to remain until Night Sister came to see me. I stood surrounded by my suitcases and waited patiently. It occurred to me that I had done a great deal of waiting since my arrival in England less than twenty-four hours ago, and I wondered whether this was going to be a pattern for the future.

I heard firm footsteps approaching from a distant corridor, and a tiny light flickered along the wooden panels. It was Night Sister. She was stern, forthright, and upright in stature.. Her stare was unfriendly as she said, "You are late, Nurse. You will have to sleep in the sick bay tonight. Wait here whilst I get the keys and a porter to take your suitcases." We eventually climbed the stairs to the room where I was installed for the night and, with a curt "I will see you in the morning", Night Sister retreated and I fell into a deep sleep.

I heard the door creak. The room was dark. Through heavy bleary eyes, I saw a stately form wearing a blue long-sleeved dress with white cuffs, over which was a sparkling white apron. A frilly white cap was perched squarely on its head. I had no idea where I was, for it was quite dark outside.

The stately form strode purposefully towards my bed, carrying something in its hand. The form stopped, and in a penetratingly commanding voice, said, "Nurse, it is time to get up. I have brought you a cup of tea. You can get dressed, and I will send you one of your friends to show you the way to the dining room and Home Sister's office."

"Nurse? One of your friends? Home Sister? Where am I? And who are you?"

"Don't be so silly, Nurse. I am the Night Sister. You arrived here rather late last night, and I had to put you in the nurses' sick bay to sleep."

It was all very confusing. I felt dehumanised, for I was suddenly stripped of my identity and of the name that was given to me at birth. And to compound it all, I was given friends whom I had never met. My mouth was dry. No words came. I need not have worried, for Night Sister turned on her heels and disappeared from the room before I could blink.

Was it only twenty-four hours ago that I had arrived at Plymouth on the SS *Antilles*? Was it only yesterday that I had taken a train to Paddington, been met by British Council, been taken to Liverpool Street Station, and settled on the 9.18 p.m. train to Colchester? Was it only last night that I had arrived at the main entrance of the hospital about midnight and had rung the bell, rattled the chains, and been eventually let in with the rebuke?

Yes, it was only last night that I stood in the cold and dimly lit main lobby of the nurses' home to await the Night Sister's arrival and her interrogation. Last night my name was Shirla. This morning I had become "Nurse"; no wonder I was confused. I sat up in the bed, reached for the cup, and had my first drink in the twenty-four hours since the SS *Antilles* docked in Plymouth Harbour.

Night Sister kept her word. My unknown friend Nurse Ambrose, a third-year nurse from Trinidad, arrived in the sick bay to escort me along the narrow, dark, and somewhat dreary corridor to the dining room.

The dining room was laid for breakfast. I had never before seen so many people dressed in nurses' uniform sitting in a room. I was not wearing a uniform, so as we entered, heads turned and eyes inspected my appearance. It was an unnerving experience. Nurse Ambrose conducted me to the table at the far end of the room to join the new intake of nurses. She explained that each table represented the level of seniority. The table nearest the entrance was for the qualified staff nurses. And the thought occurred to me that I would have a long journey before I would arrive at that eminent place.

The table for the new entrants was set for twelve. These twelve nurses had already spent two weeks in the Preliminary Training School (PTS); I was a late arrival. Kara, a kind, attractive, self-effacing maid of Italian origin, quickly added another place. Of the twelve diners, two were of West Indian origin and came from Jamaica. I was not introduced, no one acknowledged my presence, and no one's eyes met mine. I felt like a novice who had joined a silent order as I said my grace.

Breakfast over; my next port of call was Home Sister's office, where I was to be screened by the medical officer. Home Sister was of medium build and austere. Apart from the absence of a white apron, her uniform was identical to that of the Night Sister's. First to be scrutinized was my birth certificate. It was by now worn and torn, for I had produced it on several occasions recently in preparation for my departure from St Vincent. Home Sister adjusted her spectacles and moved towards the open window to examine the document. Then, turning towards me she asked, "Is this yours?"

"Yes, it is."

"Are you sure?"

"Yes, I am sure"

"Well, Nurse, I cannot accept this as a genuine document because it is in such poor condition. You will have to request a new one to be forwarded along with a letter signed by the Registrar to verify its authenticity."

I muttered to myself that my new life was going to be full of wretchedness in this place.

Next to receive her examination was the medical card that I had brought from the island. All appeared to be in order until Home Sister noticed that I had been immunized against yellow fever. And in an accusing tone she asked, "Why were you immunized against yellow fever? You would only require it if you were going abroad. That condition was eradicated from this country many years ago."

I replied, "The medical officer in St Vincent said that, as I was going abroad to England, it was necessary for me to have it." I received my first cold stare from Home Sister, and I realised then that I was not expected to respond. Unhappy though I felt at this time, I knew that I could not write to the family, for the response was likely to be that I had brought it upon myself and that no one had asked me to leave my home.

I left Home Sister's office for Matron's and was surprised to see that the person who had eventually opened the high iron gates the night before was now sitting in the Matron's chair. She was not at all what I had expected; I had anticipated a younger woman of a similar age and disposition as our Deaconess in St Vincent, who had arranged my acceptance to this hospital. I was still registering the shock of it all when the person in the chair said, "I am the Deputy Matron. I do believe that we share the same initials and surname. In order to avoid any mix-up of our correspondence, when you write home to your people, ask them to use your initials in reverse order."

I was bemused, but I had learnt from my brief encounter with Home Sister that I was not expected to respond, so I remained silent. I do not recall much of the meeting with the Deputy Matron, but I was grateful to her for agreeing that I could join the new intake of nurses now in the Preliminary Training School (PTS), despite my late arrival.

The nurses' home, where the PTS nurses were housed, was not located within the main hospital precinct. The house was a three-storied one. I occupied Room 7 on the third floor, and the two Jamaican nurses occupied Room 9. They were inseparable, and throughout the three months in PTS, we seldom spoke. The English nurses went home each weekend, leaving the three of us to our own device. We would pass one another on our way to the dining room without a flicker of recognition, and for me that was another strange experience that I found difficult to understand.

In my island at that time, politeness, personal conduct, and family background were the main criteria for acceptability. I was perturbed to discover that not only in this country but also in Jamaica; the colour of one's skin was of greater significance. Once that was explained to me, the behaviour of my two colleagues was no longer so perplexing.

Although in the later months we were allocated to the same wards and had to work together, my relationship with these two nurses remained distant. Their behaviour did not go unnoticed by the senior nurses from the West Indies. They extended the hand of friendship to me, something that was unheard of in the hierarchy of the nursing profession. In those days, senior nurses did not fraternise with junior nurses as they do today.

The weekends would have been unbearably lonely had it not been for Miss Potter's intervention. Miss Potter was the headmistress of a girls' school. She lived with her widowed mother in a pretty cottage in a village nearby. She was a friend of our Deaconess in St Vincent and had been asked to 'keep an eye on me'. On Sunday afternoons, they would take me for drives along the country lanes and villages before returning to their home where we had tea and freshly baked cream cakes.. Sadly, as the years have gone by, and with the many moves I have made in the furtherance of my career, I have lost touch with them..

As the weeks went by, I made friends with the English nurses in the PTS, and spent several happy and enjoyable weekends with their families. It was with Joanna's family that I spent the first weekend. They lived in a somewhat remote village in Suffolk. I attended the annual village fête on the Saturday afternoon. I was looking forward to enjoying myself. It had not occurred to me that my visit would create such a stir amongst the villagers. Some children screamed when they saw me; others hid behind their parents. My host, noticing the excitement that my presence had engendered, stayed close at hand and apologised with embarrassment whilst I observed in stunned silence the reactions of those who were present.

Thirteen weeks in the Preliminary Training School with my other twelve colleagues soon came to an end. I had learnt to make beds with enveloped corners and to ensure that the central fold of the counterpane ran longitudinally in the centre of the bed and that the wheels of the bed were turned inward in a straight line and free from fluff. I had practiced on models and learnt to sit them upright and surround them with pillows to ensure that they appeared comfortable. I was not convinced that real patients would derive comfort in that position, so whenever patients told me that they were more comfortable lying on their sides or lying so low under the bed covers that their heads were barely visible, I gave them the benefit of the doubt.

I could recite all the nursing procedures parrot-fashion, for Sister Tutor expected her instruction – "Screen the bed and explain the procedure to the patient" – to be regurgitated verbatim. And although I wanted to ask what was I to do if the patient were completely deaf and did not speak English, I had learnt from previous encounters with Home Sister that questions were not welcomed unless invited, and an invitation was rarely extended to new recruits. So whenever I prepared a patient for a blanket bath, I would hear the voice of Sister Tutor as a trigger and I responded as programmed.

At the end of the thirteen weeks in the Preliminary Training School, my name was added to the list of nurses who worked on a convalescent ward that was not at the main hospital but was located a half an hour's drive away. The transport left promptly at 7.00 a.m. I found this to be particularly problematic, for I had come from the West Indies where time was a languid affair; my heart sank at the thought of getting out of bed at such an ungodly hour.

The convalescent ward had two wings, the West and the East. Male patients occupied the West and female the East. Sister Pelma, who was of German origin, was in charge. It was my first encounter with someone from Germany. Coming from a West Indian island that was part of the British Empire during the war with Germany, I was instinctively afraid of her. I was also surprised that a German was allowed to live and work in England.

Back at home, we had been told that the English and the Germans were sworn enemies, as Hitler wanted to rule England and the Empire. And if he were to succeed in doing so, he would send his submarines and planes to destroy us. We already had the experience of a liner that was torpedoed in the harbour in St Lucia – one of the Windward islands – killing one of our Methodist ministers, who was a passenger returning to England. For us as children in those days, Germans were to be feared, and Hitler's Face, a popular lollypop was to be eaten with relish.

My fear of Sister Pelma was obvious, for I behaved like a timid pussycat that was afraid of its shadow. I made sure that we were never in the same wing of the ward at the same time. I was partnered with Nurse Frye who was told to show me the ropes and, show me the ropes she did. Nurse Frye had her own interpretation of the rigid procedures that I had learnt over the past thirteen weeks.

"No, you do not lay up a trolley for the blanket baths. Just give the patients water in a stainless-steel bowl and draw the curtains. They will call you when they are ready to have their backs washed."

"No, you do not lay up a trolley for rubbing patients backs; just walk around with the jar of zinc and castor oil cream, tell them to keel over, and slap it on."

In retrospect, the convalescent ward was an easy one. Apart from Mr Prince, who remained in bed, the other patients were mobile. Sister Pelma must have forgotten that the war had ended and food rationing had ceased, for she continued to dilute the milk, mix the sugar with glucose, and limit the amount of butter that we were allowed to use for the patients. Instead of cotton wool, we used Towe. At lunchtime Sister served the meals and the nurses made sure that the patients ate. On one occasion I was told to ask Mr Prince what he would like to have for his dessert. Mr Prince had replied, "Nurse, I have a pine" In St Vincent, a pineapple was often referred to as pine, so when I told Sister that the patient wanted pine for his dessert, she looked at me with disbelief, as if that confirmed her suspicion that I was really quite daft. She dispatched Nurse Frye to enquire. She returned with the response that Mr Price had a pain and wanted something to relieve it. I felt embarrassed; until then I had prided myself that I spoke and understood the English language perfectly. How wrong I was.

Six weeks of practicing my nursing skills under Nurse Frye's supervision was full of fun but damaging to the development of my professional competence. So, when my name was once more on a list to be transferred, this time to a male surgical ward on night duty, I became anxious, for I had heard that the Sister expected high standards of her nurses.

On night duty there were only two nurses. Lights were switched off at 9.30 p.m., and all the patients were expected to be tucked up comfortably in bed before Night Sister began her rounds at ten o'clock. I was referred to as the slow coach and was a source of irritation to the senior nurse. As the junior nurse, I was responsible for cleaning the sterilizer, refilling it, and having it boiled, in readiness for the day staff.

One night we were particularly busy with emergencies, and I forgot to clean the sterilizer. The following evening as we arrived on duty, there was a young black doctor sitting and chatting with Sister in her office. I noted that there was a display of spigots, pieces of cotton wool, and rubber bungs on her desk. Sister gave us the report, and then, turning to me, she asked, "Nurse Allen, did you clean the sterilizer last night?"

"Yes, Sister," was my dishonest reply.

Pointing to the array of litter on her desk, she said, "How then do you account for these?"

"I don't know, Sister."

"Mr Adler, our Ward Auxiliary, found these floating in the sterilizer this morning." With a cold and piercing stare she continued, "You will have to go to see Matron in her office tomorrow to explain."

Crestfallen, I had forgotten the presence of the young doctor, when suddenly he turned to me and asked "What did you say your name was?"

"Nurse Allen," I replied.

"Where are you from?"

I thought that he was inquisitive, but by now I had learnt that junior nurses were expected to be respectful to their seniors, so I responded meekly, "I am from St Vincent in the West Indies."

"St Vincent is a small island; you must know my wife. She has the same surname as you do. Her name is Angela."

"Angela?" I repeated. "Yes, we are related."

I knew that Angela had won a scholarship to study in England but in my excitement to leave St Vincent, I had not thought of getting an address

"I am Francis, her husband. We have just had a baby; Donna is her name. We live just across the road from the hospital. You must come to see us. I will tell her to expect you."

49

I got no sympathy from the senior nurse. In fact, she was particularly bullying that night. So, I made sure that the sterilizer was thoroughly cleaned; the inner basket removed, and the debris cleared. The thought of going to Matron's office was demoralizing, and I dreaded the morning. But it soon came. We handed over the report to Sister, and as I was about to leave, she said, "Nurse, I want you to show me the sterilizer." We walked towards the sterilizing room; she examined it, nodded, and said, "You have done well, Nurse. You don't have to go to Matron after all."

Why the change of mind? I thought. Was it the clean sterilizer or was it Dr Francis?

Chapter 4:
Adjusting to Life in England

It had become apparent in the early days that life as a student nurse would not be an easy one for those of us who came from the West Indian islands with an almost missionary approach to life, with noble ideals and a passionate desire to minister to the sick.

In the late '50s and early '60s, most people appeared to be intrigued by the presence of West Indian nurses within the hospital. We were viewed as being partly mysterious and partly exotic. During my first few months on the wards, I was asked on several occasions the same questions by patients and visitors alike. And always in deliberately slow speech and with exaggerated pronunciation, "Nurse, how long have you been in England?"

"Three months," I had replied.

"Did you learn to speak it since you came here?"

"No, I did not."

"Where did you learn to speak such good English?" they had asked.

And I had answered, "In St Vincent. Everyone speaks English there."

"Do they?" they asked with genuine surprise.

I had felt that these questions were a sign of their preconceived ideas and low expectations of us. I learnt later that many within the profession also held similar views.

I found my three months as a junior on night duty to be disorientating. At our hospital, nurses on night duty worked a schedule of twelve hours each night and four consecutive nights per week. On the busy male surgical ward, where I worked, I dreaded the ring of the telephone, for invariably it meant an emergency admission and preparation for the operating theatre. On some occasions we were so busy that we were obliged to work without a break.

I told myself that it was character forming. So I applied all the diligence, good humour, and stamina that I could muster. By the light of a torch, I carried out and recorded the routine observations necessary for the safe recovery of the post-operative patients. Apart from the occasional barking of instructions, the senior nurse ignored my presence.

At the end of the three months, as I had succeeded in doing the patients no harm, I considered that I had fulfilled the expectations of Florence Nightingale. That, however, was not the perception of the senior nurse, and an unflattering account of my abilities was widely reported amongst her colleagues. So I was pleased when my name was once more on the list to return to day duty. This time I was to work on a gynaecological ward.

There was a light-hearted atmosphere on the gynaecological ward. Most of the patients were young, full of fun, and admitted only for short periods. Unlike my experience on the convalescent ward with Nurse Frye and Sister Pelma, I learnt once more to practice nursing the way I had been taught in the Preliminary Training School. I felt at ease with the patients and staff.

I got to know the patients and relatives quite well. Many of them extended invitations on their discharge. I accepted, promised to visit, but never did. There was one patient who was not prepared to take no for an answer. Her husband was a headmaster of a grammar school in a neighbouring seaside resort. It must have been the lure of the sea that I had not seen since my arrival that made me accept the invitation.

Their house was one of a terrace. It had high ceilings and old-fashioned wallpaper and carpets that matched. There was a warm and inviting coal fire burning in the room they referred to as the front parlour. They introduced me to their neighbours, who viewed me with friendly curiousity. On the Saturday morning, we walked along the promenade and I realised that the sea was not as warm and inviting as it was at home, but I was pleased to renew my acquaintance as I shivered in the embracing breeze.

During the evening I met with some of the other teachers socially. It was quite a lively occasion, but at a certain stage I realised that I was an object of study. I also became a little perturbed at some of the views that were being expressed about the inferior intellectual capacity of people from the black Commonwealth.

Initially, I tried to dispel the misconceptions, but they invested me with a chip on my shoulder. I realised that I was not expected to influence their long-held views, erroneous though they were. Any attempt to do so would be misguided. The experience of that weekend had a profound effect on me. I decided that the time had come for me to make radical adjustments and to reappraise my view of the new world to which I had now become a part.

At times like this, I have found my natural inclination is to retreat to my inner resources, to draw upon my early childhood experience – back to the days when I played with the rocks and the stones by the seashore. I became more reflective and valued the opportunity to have my own space, to be left alone with my thoughts, to be selective with whom I shared those thoughts, to be friendly but not familiar, and to establish a boundary that was invisible to others but within which I felt comfortable.

Even if I had wished to be more sociable, the opportunities to be so were limited. As nurses we worked unsociable hours. We had few recreational facilities and were low-paid. When we did go out we would visit the local subterranean coffee bar. This bar became a very popular and affordable dive for us student nurses, as a cup of coffee cost six pence – the equivalent of today's two and a half pence. We could drink there and be extravagant on a salary of eight pounds and twelve pence per month.

There were, of course, the pubs. The one nearest to the hospital was referred to as Ward 8 because it was frequented by the young doctors who were on call. Most of the local student nurses were either engaged or going steady and were busy saving for their trousseau and wedding. Unlike today, there were no universities in the area so the opportunity for the student nurses to socialise with other students was limited.

On the occasions when the hospital organised its own social function, invitations were extended to the staff at the British Military Hospital in the area and to the local police. In those early days, nurses from the West Indies did not find these events to be the fun that they were meant to be, especially as they did not have their own escorts. Although rock and roll, the jive, and the twist were popular amongst the young people of the day, the orchestra, under the watchful eyes of the Matron and Home Sister, played tunes that included the waltz and fox trot, neither of which inspired the West Indian nurses.

Later, when we were allowed to invite staff at the American bases in Suffolk and Norfolk, American GIs became regular guests at the functions. Airmen, with their exuberant mannerisms, brought vibrancy to the occasions, and this appealed to all the nurses. Those from the West Indies began to participate fully and to derive as much enjoyment from the events as everyone else. Even the orchestra began to experiment with the music of the day, much to Home Sister's displeasure.

My placement on the gynaecological ward came to an end after three months. It was time for a change. Once more the list of names appeared, and mine was included with those who were entitled to a fortnight's leave. Leave at the County meant leaving the County. But I knew no one. Where was I to go?

I remembered being told by our Deaconess in St Vincent that there was a Methodist International House (MIH) in Inverness Terrace, Bayswater in London that catered for overseas students. So there I went. I had driven through London to Liverpool Street Station on the night I had arrived in England, but I did not consider that I had been to London. This fortnight was going to be full of new experiences for me and I was looking forward to it.

In the late 1950s MIH – as it was fondly referred to by the students – was a safe and friendly place. There were students from various parts of the Commonwealth. A number of them came from the newly independent state of Ghana. They exuded confidence and optimism. I had not met any one from Africa before. I was fascinated by their elegance and the flamboyance of their clothes. Although it felt generally good to be amongst them, I was saddened on the occasions when it was necessary for me to challenge their views about the heritage and capabilities of West Indians and their links to slavery. They held the genuine belief that, unlike the West Africans who were mainly students, those of us who came from the West Indians were ill-educated immigrants, recruited only for our labouring skills.

I shared a room with two sisters who were from St Kitts, part of the Leeward Island group. They were nursing in the Burnley. We teamed up to see the sights of London and enjoyed the excitement of travelling on the tubes, going the wrong way on the Circle Line, getting lost between the Strand and Trafalgar Square stations, and posing for photographs with the pigeons in the Square. It was a time of fun and exploration.

One day, on a visit to Lyons Corner House for tea, I thought I saw someone whom I recognised. She was wiping the tables, and she was wearing a cap and apron. It could not be the person I knew, for she came to London to do dress designing. She had been a teacher at home. She was highly qualified for that. She had a Cambridge Higher School Certificate – the then-requirement for entrance to a university. What was she doing clearing tables? I needed to be sure, so I approached her; she had obviously seen me and hoped that I did not recognise her. She burst into tears and said she could not speak to me then but promised to visit me on the following day.

She came as promised and took me to her home. On the way she tried to prepare me for what to I was about to see. She lived in one of the tenement houses that were owned by Peter Rachman, a notorious slum landlord operating in the Notting Hill and Westbourne Park areas. It was not the kind of accommodation that I had been led to believe existed in England. I was stunned that she had been reduced to living in that environment, knowing what she had left behind at home in our little island.

The entrance was strewed with litter. Cobwebs hung from the high ceiling like worn and tattered grey drapes. There was no lighting on the stairway, so tenants used torches. The smell from paraffin heaters, the only means of heating, greeted us as we entered the building. It was dark, cold, and eerie. Her home was a large room on the third floor. A light from an unshaded bulb lightened the darkness. The only furniture were a bed, a small table, an upright chair, and an armchair that was unsafe to sit on. A small recess hidden by a light curtain acted as a wardrobe.

She shared the kitchen and bathroom with other tenants on that floor. In the kitchen there was a gas cooker that they all shared. They got their gas by inserting money into a metre. It was not unknown for tenants to use another person's gas if left unattended, so she asked me to remain in the kitchen whilst she went out to the shop. I found it unnerving standing there. From time to time, the figure of a tenant would appear in the doorway of the kitchen, only to retreat when our eyes met.

How could this happen to someone who had such a bright future in the West Indies, whose parents had room enough to spare? Hers was a tale about promises that were not kept by relatives, her stubborn pride, and a feeling of failure if she were to return home without achieving her goal. So here she was, working during the day, studying at night, and imploring me not to let anyone at home know the truth. We agreed to meet again before my return to Colchester.

We did not meet, for during the following week, the Notting Hill Gate riot broke out. It had been caused by tensions between English Teddy boys and new arrivals from the West Indies. It became unsafe for me to visit her tenement. I felt relieved that I had a genuine reason for not doing so, but we kept in touch with each other. She subsequently returned home and attended the University of the West Indies before becoming a highly respected headmistress in one of the islands of the Eastern Caribbean.

The experience of spending my first holiday in London and staying at the Methodist International House in Bayswater, a stone's throw away from the Notting Hill Gate riots had a disquieting effect. I could not help questioning this notion of a race riot. How could the street fights between a relatively small number of English Teddy boys and the newly arrived West Indian men be called a race riot? Why was it called a riot? And who benefited from calling it a riot? Was this a means of encouraging ignorance, intolerance, and colour prejudice within and amongst the wider British public? There were no other races involved – No Chinese, Japanese, or Indians.

I wrestled with a feeling of disquiet. I did not want to believe that it was possible that a new form of South African apartheid or Southern American segregation was about to constrain that freedom of spirit that was inherent in West Indians. I was overcome by a deep sense of disappointment. And I felt that I was about to undergo an internal change that could be irrevocable.

The fortnight's holiday soon came to an end, and I returned to the hospital on the Sunday evening. I arrived after dark and caught the last taxi in the station. As I entered the taxi I saw two Administrative Sisters from the hospital. I thought they would not like wait in the dark, so I asked the driver to stop. I ran towards the couple to offer them a lift. The response was in their stare. They looked deeply offended. Feeling rather humiliated, I returned to the taxi and made the journey alone. A few days later, I described the encounter to Nurse Barton, an English nurse. She shook her head. "You did what?" she asked in disbelief. Then she added, "You have some learning to do."

"Learning – what learning?" I asked

"Look at it this way," she said, "You've just come out from the PTS. You are one of the most junior nurses in the hospital, and you have asked two Senior Administrative Sisters to share your taxi!"

"So?" I asked

"Don't say I didn't warn you," she replied

"Warn me about what?"

She raised her eyes heavenwards then looked at me as she said, "You are in England. You are black. What do you expect?"

Now that I had returned to the safety of the hospital and my nursing duties, I told myself that I was leaving the London experience behind. But that was not to be. I found that I could not erase from my memory the riots in Notting Hill Gate and the Peter Rachman accommodation in Westbourne Park where my friend lived. Nor could I forget the anxious faces of the other tenants as they fleetingly appeared at the kitchen door. And resounding in my ears were Nurse Barton's words of warning and the shocked expression on her face when I told her that I had offered a lift in my taxi to the Administrative Sisters.

———————

Back from my holiday, I was sent to work on a male medical ward where the sister had the reputation for being fierce and feisty, so I was not looking forward to the encounter. The ward was an L-shaped one. The nurses' station was situated at the right angle so it was easy to see the patients in both wings. There were, also on that ward, two other nurses who had started their training at the same time as I had done. They had been working on the ward for a few weeks before me. Sister acted as if she was unaware of our equal status, and I became the permanent junior nurse of the ward.

Being the junior nurse meant that I was not expected to accompany her on the doctor's rounds, nor was I permitted to dispense medicines to the patients. In fact, my role as the junior nurse was restricted to what was euphemistically referred to as the "Four B's", beds, baths, bedpans, and backs.

There was nothing inspiring about this role. And after an initial four weeks on the ward, I had learnt nothing. The other two nurses were being exposed to many learning experiences in preparation for the Preliminary Examination that we were expected to sit in the following two months. My repeated attempts to remind Sister that I was there to learn and that I needed relevant practical experience to pass my exam fell on deaf ears. The final straw came on a day when one of my colleagues said, "Nurse, Sister says you are to go to the autoclave to collect a drum of sterile towels and another of sterile dressings for me to lay up a trolley for the Consultant's rounds."

Gently, I responded, "I suggest that you get it yourself."

When Sister heard of my response, her reaction was immediate. And in her most authoritative tone of voice, she shouted, "Nurse, go to Matron's office at once." I did not go to see the Matron. Instead, I went to the Post Office and sent a telegram home to St Vincent, saying, "Money for Return Passage Urgently Needed."

That done, I returned to the nurses' home, tied my uniform in a neat bundle, packed my suitcases, locked the door, and awaited the response to my telegram. It was not surprising to me that my absence from the ward went unnoticed, for the afternoons were the time that relatives came to visit.

It was 3.30 p.m. when I heard the Home Sister's voice at my door.

"Nurse," she shouted as she tried to turn the door handle "You should be on duty. Sister is looking for you to perform last offices on a patient. I sighed deeply at the thought, for this was one of those unpleasant tasks that a nurse is expected to undertake. It entailed the preparing of a dead patient for the morgue.

Still rattling the door handle, she barked, "Nurse, will you please open this door at once?"

Slowly I unlocked the door, and Home Sister entered. She surveyed my surroundings and, in an even sterner voice enquired, "What is this all about, Nurse?"

I responded calmly, "I am going home. I have sent for my passage, my suitcases are packed, and the uniform is folded in that bundle."

Home Sister must have thought that I had flipped my lid, for she said in a softer tone, "Now, Nurse, please put on your uniform, and I will escort you to the ward. Sister is waiting for you."

Defeated, I did as I was told, and like an escaped convict, Home Sister escorted me to the ward and passed me over to my gaoler who handed down my punishment – I was to perform the last offices on a patient with the help of an auxiliary nurse. Meekly, I went off to do the task.

The hospital's grapevine was an efficient one. By suppertime, everyone had heard that I had been frog-marched by Home Sister, but no one asked why. I was aware of the murmurs and stares as I entered the dining room, but no one spoke to me, and I was pleased to return to the peacefulness of my room at the end of the day.

But my peace was to be interrupted once again – this time it was Night Sister. She sounded anxious and excited as she knocked at my door and called my name. She entered, waving a telegram, and demanded an explanation.

I replied, "I am going home. I sent a telegram this morning for money to pay my passage, and I believe this is the response." So, stretching my hand out for it, I read its contents which said

"LETTER MONEY FOLLOWING RELAX LOVE PAULINE"

"You cannot leave us like that, Nurse. It will reflect badly on the hospital. I will get some of your friends to come and talk you out of this decision."

I said nothing, for I remembered that just over a year ago it was Night Sister who had greeted me on my arrival from St Vincent, had called me Nurse, and had given me friends whom I had not met before and whom I could not have known, and I felt that history was about to repeat itself. It was quite late at night, but Night Sister was able to find a flurry of West Indian nurses, whom she sent to my room to persuade me to change my mind.

Nurse Layton, a nurse from Jamaica, was the most senior of the nurses who came to my room that night. She was held in high regard by the ward sisters and junior nurses. Sitting on my bed and holding my hand as if she were a wise counsellor, she said, "I know how you are feeling. Similar things have happened to all of us. If you want to get on in this hospital and to get your State Registration, you have to learn how to stoop to conquer."

I withdrew my hand from her hold, and looking directly at her, I asked, "Stoop? How low?"

In the event, it was not the nurses who succeeded but it was the Matron who did. For when I went to her office the following morning, instead of standing with my hands behind my back and facing a stern figure seated behind a desk, she said, pointing to one of her armchairs, "Do have a seat, Nurse."

Surprised, I looked around to see if there were someone else in the room, but there was no one else, so I warily did as I was told. Matron left her desk to occupy the other armchair. I became even more guarded. She poured two cups of coffee from a tray and offered me one. I thought, this is strange. What game is she going to play this time?

"Well, Nurse – Do you have something to say to me?"

"No, Matron."

"Night Sister tells me that you are planning to return home without completing your training."

"Yes, Matron.

"Can I ask the reason?"

"I think that you already know."

"No, Nurse, I want you to tell me in your own words why you have made the decision to leave us in this manner."

"I am not getting the practical nursing experience I need to pass my exam. Sister is constantly shouting at me in front of the patients, which makes me look incompetent. I am given all the unpleasant duties that an auxiliary would normally perform."

Matron breathed deeply, then said, "Nurse, I would like you to reconsider your decision. You have already completed eighteen months of your training. It would be a disappointment to your family if you were to return home without completing the entire course."

"I know that I have completed the eighteen months of my training, but I have not had the practical experience that is required for my Nursing Exams, and I am unlikely to pass. I feel as if I have wasted the previous year of training, and that makes me unhappy. I have contacted my family at home, and they have sent the money for my passage."

"It would reflect badly on the hospital if you were to leave for the reason you have stated. It would also affect the morale of the other nurses from your country who have just started their training. I wish you would reconsider, and I will speak with Sister. Think about it for a week or two, and then come back to me if you really are determined to leave."

I wish I knew what Matron said to the Sister, for from that day, I had no further difficulties. I earned the right to be treated with respect and to be given the same opportunity as the other student nurses within the hospital. Life became bearable, and I settled down to complete my training and to qualify as a State Registered Nurse.

The last eighteen months of my training at the County went very quickly, and I was now within weeks of sitting the State Final Exam. I had no sooner passed the Preliminary Exam than I had found myself scheduled for two periods on night duty as the senior nurse. The first was to be responsible for a female medical ward and the second for the paediatric unit.

During the period that followed Matron's intervention in resolving my unhappy experience on the male medical ward, Sister's attitude towards me had changed. I was finally included in her teaching sessions and learnt a great deal about most medical conditions and their treatment. I felt confident to take on the role of senior night nurse for the female medical ward. And remembering my experience as a junior nurse, I resolved not to expose others to a similar fate. So the junior nurse and I developed an easy professional relationship, where we worked together as a pair with the shared objective of caring for our patients and ensuring that they came to no harm.

When the time came for me to take charge of the paediatric unit I disgraced myself, for I had not worked with children before. The thought of being in charge of a ward where there were babies and toddlers who could not speak was terrifying. I tried in vain to express my anxiety to the Administrative Sisters but rules were rules, and in their estimation, I had reached the level of seniority where I was expected to be able to deal with any eventuality.

But that was not how I felt. So on the first night that I was due to be on duty, I was filled with terror. I imagined having to care for screaming children, dealing with emergencies, and not knowing where to find equipment. In a highly emotional state, I went to Night Sister's office, burst into tears and stuttered, "I can't do it. I can't do it; they will all be dead by morning. I don't know where anything is, and they can't speak to me. I can't do it."

"Don't be so silly. You are a third-year nurse. Surely you can cope on the children's ward."

"No, I can't, and I won't go on that ward. Send me somewhere else."

My distress must have registered, for I was sent off duty with the instruction that I was to present myself on the paediatric unit the following morning, where I was to work for a month. And following that period, I was to assume the responsibility for the unit as the senior nurse on night duty. With great relief I went back to the nurses' home, had a good night's sleep, and reported for duty the following morning. Once again the hospital's grapevine was busy, for when I arrived on the ward I was greeted by Sister and the staff nurse, with the words: "So we hear you are afraid of children?"

"Not afraid. I am just terrified."

We all laughed, and they made sure that by the end of the period I was no longer terrified but confident to care for the little ones. Nursing the patients on the paediatric ward became a most enjoyable experience. There were twenty-four on the ward. Each member of staff had her own group of four children to care for. We were not only the nurse but also the substitute mother.

This was the 1960s, when there was a rigid approach to hospital visiting hours, and for the paediatric unit, there was no exemption. A bell summoned the visitors when it was time to enter, and it rang again twice at five-minute intervals as a warning that the visiting was soon to end. This was usually an emotional time with tearful goodbyes.

The month's experience on the paediatric ward had given me the confidence I needed when it was time for me to become the senior nurse on night duty. I had learnt a great deal and was able to transfer some of my knowledge to the junior nurse who worked with me. It was while I was on the paediatric ward that I sat the written and practical parts of the State Registration Exam.

Six weeks after my practical exam, I received a letter informing me that my name would be placed on the General Nursing Council's Register for State Registered Nurses in the United Kingdom, on the payment of three Guineas. This brought me up with a jolt, for I suddenly realised that I had come to the end of a road and decisions had to be made.

I had left St Vincent to undertake my nurses' training, and that was now completed. I had made no plans for the future, nor had I really seriously considered nursing as a career. Coming to England to undertake the training had been an acceptable reason for leaving home. But I had never considered remaining in England on a long-term basis as a possible option. Now, here I was at the end of my training and facing a wide and open road that could lead me to oblivion if I did not take positive action. But I had no idea what form this positive action should take.

I have found over the years that nurses are very good at offering unsolicited advice, and I received plenty of that from Nurse James and Nurse Houghton. Both had qualified six months before and had opted to stay on as Staff Nurses. Now they were moving on to undertake their midwifery training at the Glasgow Royal Infirmary.

They came to my room in the nurses' home, carrying a bottle of ginger wine. "We've come to celebrate with you," they said

Surprised but pleased, I replied, "That's nice of you."

Sitting cross-legged on the floor, Nurse Houghton asked, "So, Girl, what are you going to do now?"

"Oh, I am going home," I replied.

"What are you going to do when you get there?" she asked. Then, wagging her index finger, she explained, "You can't go back home to the West Indies without a Midwifery qualification. You would only be half a nurse if you went back without it. The nurses down there would laugh at you. All nurses in the West Indies have to care for pregnant women and deliver their babies. They even apply forceps and put up intravenous infusions. Come to Glasgow with us; at least you will be able to see another part of the country."

The euphoria I had experienced from passing the exam was slowly ebbing away, for I possessed none of the skills she described. My confidence took a serious nosedive. I had no desire to go further north, where I had heard that it was always cold and bleak. Furthermore, I had ruled out any thought of Scotland, for I had heard that it snowed most of the year. In any case, Scotland was another country, and I had left home for England.

Whilst I was dithering about my next move, Matron introduced a policy that meant that the hospital badge would not be awarded to nurses who did not remain at the County for a further six months following the successful completion of their training. This gave me time to think more clearly about my future career, so I decided to opt for the six-month Operating Theatre Course that the hospital was offering to qualified nurses. It also provided me with the valid reason for not going to Glasgow with the two nurses. A week later, when they were leaving the hospital, their parting advice to me was: "If you don't come to Glasgow, then go to a hospital in the East End of London. You would get a lot of experience delivering babies. They drop them like flies down there."

I made a mental note of this and decided to submit an application to Hackney Maternity Hospital, located in the Homerton area of the Borough of Hackney.

Chapter 5:
Midwifery in London

I left Essex for London to attend an interview at Hackney Hospital. It was 1962. The hospital was once an old workhouse. There were large iron gates, and beyond them stood the grey stone walls of the hospital that was to become my place of work and my home for the next nine months. The head porter was at the entrance. He was reading a newspaper. Pausing, I said, "Good morning. Can you show me the way to Matron's office?"

Without acknowledging me, he waved his hand in a vague direction. Not understanding what he meant, I repeated my question. He looked up, stared at me, then shouted at a man who was sweeping, and said

"Hey, Jock, show your friend the way to Matron's office!"

I gave him a stony stare, which Jock must have observed, for he intervened by saying, "Young lady, don't bother with him. He is ignorant. In fact, they are all ignorant in this place." He left his task, walked towards me and asked, "Are you a nurse?"

"Yes, I am."

"Are you coming to work here?"

"Yes," I replied

"This is not the place for you. You must not stay here too long. You would get demoralised. Nurses who stay here don't get anywhere."

Jock was from Montserrat, an island in the West Indies. He was, as I later discovered, a highly educated man, who was employed as a sweeper. He directed me to the Matron's office. Matron's office was a large room situated off a long dark corridor. The room was stark and unpainted. The only attempt to brighten the walls consisted of a framed portrait of the Queen Mother and a reproduction of the famous image of Florence Nightingale holding a lamp. The building looked and felt like a workhouse.

Matron was a woman of slender build, with high cheekbones and thin lips. Her lips seemed to have lost the ability and will to smile. Her thinning grey hair was parted in the centre and secured in a bun at the back. Her spectacles were perched on the edge of her nose. An upright wooden chair was placed on the other side of her desk, where she beckoned me to sit. Her blue eyes stared penetratingly at me as if to read my thoughts. The interview was brief. There was the mandatory scrutiny of my State Registration Certificate, followed by an agreed starting date; and an assurance that I would be given a room in the nurses' home during my midwifery training. I was then dismissed.

The conversation with Jock and the Matron, in addition to the stark surroundings of the workhouse made me ask myself, Had I made a mistake in coming to Hackney? If I had, there was no turning back, for I had already resigned from the County Hospital.

The midwifery course started at the end of September, so I was offered a Staff Nurse's post on a paediatric ward throughout the summer of 1962. Hackney in the 1960s was not like Colchester. Its population included a large number of people from different parts of the world. In Colchester I nursed only English patients, so I was not prepared for the cultural mix that Hackney presented.

Dust, smoke, and poor housing conditions meant that children were admitted for routine tonsillectomies, chest infections, and other minor ailments that would normally be dealt with at home. As part of the admissions procedure, the children had to be screened for nits. And if found, they were to be treated. The treatment included shampooing, applying an anti-nit solution, and bandaging the head. I had not treated any patients with nits in Colchester.

The parents, especially the mothers, were very different from the parents that I had met during my training. In Hackney, they tended to wear tightly fitted short skirts and shoes with stiletto heels. Their hair was often bleached blonde and set in the style of a beehive. When the mothers arrived at visiting time and found their children's head had been bandaged, they were extremely embarrassed. Embarrassment invariably turned to hostility that was supported by a tirade of verbal abuse and foul language. The tirade was directed at the nursing staff. This behaviour did not ever occur in Colchester and would not have been tolerated there.

I soon realised the limitations of my training, as I had not been exposed to different cultures or faiths. This put me at a disadvantage when caring for the people in Hackney. The Borough had a mixed population with a substantial Jewish community. I had no knowledge of Jewish cultural values or practices, and though I had been accustomed to dealing with Hospital Chaplains, I had never met a Rabbi.

My first encounter with Jewish culture came when a young boy was admitted with a fractured femur. I went into a complete spin when his father brought in his own cutlery and crockery. He must have thought that I was most uncooperative, for I tried to explain that there was no need for him to do so, as the hospital provided for all its patients. As we seemed to be talking at cross-purposes and getting nowhere, I sought the assistance of the Sister on a nearby ward, who explained why he had bought his own cutlery.

From September onwards, I was very busy. Unlike the present time, the contraceptive pill was not routinely available, and there were high rates of pregnancy in the Borough. Most of the new arrivals who had settled there were of childbearing age. There was a policy of home delivery, and the District Midwives were asked to visit the home to make an assessment of the living conditions. They reported that the poor housing situation that existed meant that it was unsuitable for women to be delivered in their own homes. So they came to the hospital's maternity unit in Hackney.

My six months at the maternity unit was very demanding and stressful. This was the time that a number of babies were being born with deformities, resulting from their mothers having taken Thalidomide, a drug that was meant to moderate the effects of morning sickness during the early months of pregnancy. The unit was so busy at nights that we were often unable to spare the time that was necessary to comfort, console, and counsel these mothers. The words "dropping them like flies" kept on reverberating in my ears. Personally, I would have preferred fewer flies to be dropped and more time for comfort and support. This was the most distressing aspect of my work.

I learnt the key words for "Push" in the various languages in order to ensure the safe delivery of babies. I also learnt how to work with women from all over the world who had different expectations, fears and hopes about giving birth in a foreign country where the people spoke a language that was different from their mother tongue.

Living and working in Hackney had exposed me to a way of life that I had not experienced before, and I knew instinctively that I could not continue to work in or live there beyond the length of the training. I felt restricted, for there was very little opportunity to do anything other than deliver babies. The popular television programmes for the nurses were *Emergency Ward 10* and the early episodes of *Coronation Street,* neither of which appealed to me. There were no local underground station,s and the only bus that served the area stopped running at 11.00 p.m. I found that it was virtually impossible to visit Central London and to spend an evening at a concert or at the theatre.

Although I did get a wide range of experience and at the end of the period, I had delivered over thirty babies, I knew that I needed to escape to another place, where I could relax and enjoy my training. It was a conversation that I had with a Senior Midwife that confirmed my decision to move on was the right one. The Midwife managed the labour unit at night. I had been shadowing her for a fortnight, when out of the blue she asked, "Nurse, what do you intend to do when you've qualified as a midwife?"

Surprised at the question, I replied, "I am planning to go home."

"Good!" she said with some emotion.

"Why good?" I asked.

"Look at me," she said bitterly. "I've been working in this hospital for six years. I have twice applied for a Sister's post. The first time they gave it to somebody from outside because they said that she had more experience than me. Today I went for an interview and do you know what? They have given the post to one of my former students."

"Oh," I said, feigning surprise – for I remembered Jock's words of warning: "Don't stay here too long, because you won't get anywhere."

"Have you thought of trying another hospital?" I enquired.

"I will now!" she said. Then, reflecting for a while, she shook her head and continued, "You know, Nurse; you can never win in this place. You try to make progress and they knock you back every time. Take for instance my husband and me. We've saved regularly with the Bank for the past six years, but when we went to get a loan to buy a house, they told us that we didn't qualify for one because we were Bank customers for less than ten years. That wasn't what they told my neighbour, who got a loan even though she didn't have an account with them."

"So what did you do?" I asked.

"We did what people used to do at home when they wanted to raise a big sum of money – We threw a partner."

Puzzled, I repeated her words. "Threw a partner? What do you mean?"

She flung her head back and chuckled, then replied, "Don't tell me you've never heard about that. It is a popular way for a group of people to raise money for a down payment on a property or any big expenditure if they don't have enough savings. All you have to do is to get between twelve and twenty individuals to join together to save £5.00 or £10.00 per week. Each week one member would be given the total sum collected, and that would serve as an initial deposit. That is the way that most of we West Indians become able to buy our own homes in this country."

"Oh," I responded lamely. But I was grateful for this information.

I had made one good friend at the hospital. We were pupils on the same midwifery course at the Maternity Hospital. Sally was of West Indian origin; tall, slim, attractive, and she succeeded in always looking elegant, even in a nurse's uniform. Her long black hair was arranged in a bun well above the nape of her neck and was in line with the centre of the nurse's cap. Her blue uniform rested just below the knees. She entered the dining room on the first day of the course as if she were modelling the uniform. She paused at the table where I was seated, surveyed it briefly, and decided that I was worthy of her company.

Our eyes met in a blank stare. I noticed that her makeup had been perfectly applied; her natural eyebrows had been replaced by a strategically crafted pair that was positioned just a little higher than it should normally have been. This was our first meeting, and I was overcome with an uncontrollable urge to be mischievous. So smilingly, I asked, "Nurse, did you have an accident with your eyebrows?"

Her response was colourful and delivered in a Jamaican accent. I said nothing. My reaction to her diatribe must have puzzled her, for she stopped suddenly and, staring at me, asked, "What part of Jamaica you come from?"

"Oh," I said "I am not from Jamaica. I am from St Vincent."

"Where is that?" she said.

"One of the Windward Islands."

With a dismissive wave of her hand, she scoffed, "Small island."

Shaking my head, I said, "Small and beautiful just like me." She laughed, and the tension was released. We became firm friends and decided that we would continue the next six months of our training in Kent.

It was in the spring of 1963 that we moved to Kent. We had just experienced the smog and one of the bitterest winters for many years. It was also the year that marked the beginning of some profound social changes in England. The media became more intrusive. There was the Profumo Affair, the emergence of Christine Keeler, a former call girl, as an icon. Cassius Clay fought Henry Cooper and won. And the West Indies beat England in the Test match at Lords. This was a good start to the year.

Sally and I were the only two midwifery students in a cottage hospital in Kent. I had forgotten that in completing the application form, I had stated that I was a cyclist; as that was a prerequisite for acceptance. At the end of the three months in the hospital, we were given bicycles and told that as the next three months would be spent in the community, we would be living in the home of a District Midwife and working under her supervision.

I was anxious on the two accounts. Sally, on the other hand, was not concerned. In fact, she had already bought a moped and had ordered an especially smart peaked helmet in keeping with her image. She rode off to the Midwife's home whilst I walked my bicycle the two miles from the hospital to our new abode.

Our District Midwife had two children. Jack, aged 13 years, was given the task of teaching me to ride; for after the first three home deliveries, supervised by the midwife, I was expected to find my own way to the client's home and to summon help only if I suspected that there was likely to be some difficulty.

The house was in a close, so with Jack's encouragement and support, it became our freeway. My attempt at learning to ride was a source of amusement for the other residents in the close. They cheered when I managed to remain upright and sighed whenever I fell, which was quite often. Jack must have been a good teacher, for I conquered the rudimentary art of cycling within three weeks. Gradually I became more confident and was soon claiming my right to share the Rochester Way with lorries and other four-wheeled vehicles.

Living in the family home of the District Midwife was my first experience of being a lodger in England. Sally and I shared a room. We were invited to "make ourselves at home". We had alternate weekends off duty and were not expected to remain in the house. I spent my weekends in London with my sister, who was undertaking her Librarianship course and was sharing a flat with another student. Sally, who was engaged to Robert, also spent her weekends in London. They were planning to marry after she had completed the course.

On those evenings when the District was quiet, we sat with the family and held wide-ranging discussions. We learnt much about the war in Europe, the effect on them as a young German-English couple, the discrimination that they had to overcome, and the banishment from relatives and friends.

Today I look back on the experience with great fondness for Sally and I were fortunate to have lived with such a liberal-minded family. Other colleagues were not so fortunate. They found that they were expected to undertake some of the household duties. And one particular student, during her off duty period, was expected to assist with the redecorating of the house.

Sally and I were very confident as newly qualified midwives. We felt that we had every reason to be, for whilst we were students, our midwife had taken leave to tour Devon with friends and had left us in charge of her home and the area. We were to call upon another midwife in a neighbouring area if we had any concerns. Thankfully, all went well and we therefore felt justified in assuming an air of self-assurance.

So it was that in September 1963, exuding self-confidence, Sally returned to London to prepare for her wedding and I presented myself at County Hall, Westminster, for an interview for the post of District Midwife (Teaching) in Islington, a part of the North London Division.

My initial impression of County Hall, situated close to Westminster Bridge on the bank of the River Thames, was that of a cold, imposing building. It was an environment completely different from the friendly home surroundings I had now left behind in Kent. Inside the building, the impersonal atmosphere was reflected in the interviewing room. A highly polished long table separated me from the three formidable-looking women in grey uniform and one man who were about to interview me. Their expressions were inscrutable. No attempt was made to put me at ease.

The interview took the form of an interrogation. At one stage I felt that I had become invisible. The panel members held an open discussion as to whether or not Mrs Beech, the supervisor of midwives for the North London Division, who was not on the panel, would be prepared to welcome me as a member of her midwifery team. I was a little perplexed at the discussion, but as they agreed to offer me the post, I dismissed my momentary bewilderment. On the date agreed, I joined a team of other new appointees. We appointees stayed in a midwives' hostel in Holloway North London. The hostel was run by Mrs Hawkins, a senior midwife. She was responsible for helping us to settle into our roles in the district.

I was given a geographical area that was close to Arsenal Football Club. I had been managing it for six weeks when I was summoned to meet the Mrs Beech. As a supervisor, she was responsible for ensuring that we were competent midwifery practitioners who followed our regulatory and statutory obligations. This was going to be our first meeting.

Her office was located off a corridor on the first floor of a civic building. A heavy wooden door bore her name and status. Instinctively, I took a deep breath, adjusted my uniform, and knocked.

"Come in," barked a voice from behind the door.

I entered. The occupant remained seated behind her desk, and as there was no other chair, I stood facing her throughout, feeling as if I had been summoned by the headmistress to apologise for a misdemeanour. Still turning the pages of a file that was in front of her, she raised her eyes, gave me a cursory glance, then asked "How long have you been qualified as a midwife?"

"Since September this year," I replied.

"Where did you gain your community experience?"

"I was placed with a midwife in Kent."

Pushing her chair slightly away from her desk and looking at me with cold grey eyes, she asked, "And do you think that your limited experience in rural Kent equips you to be a midwife in charge of a busy London area?"

"Yes," I said, and added, "The district in Kent covered a large area and was very busy. So I had the opportunity to get a lot of experience. The midwife had confidence in—" I was not allowed to complete the sentence, for the supervisor interrupted me by saying, "Never mind what the midwife in Kent said, this is London. The pace of life is faster than it is in the country. Can you drive?"

"No," I replied. "I've failed my driving test." I received another disapproving stare from my interrogator, and I began to get the distinct feeling that had she been at the interview, I would not have been her preferred candidate. It was clear that she felt I did not possess the experience that she required of her midwives. She remained silent for a few moments, as if she were considering the sentence she wished to mete out to me. At last she said, "I have discussed with a colleague who is looking for a midwife for an area in Poplar."

"Poplar! Where is that?" I asked.

"It is an area in the East End of London where there is soon to be a vacancy and where I am sure that you would be happy. There are a number of midwives from your part of the world who are working there."

Too shocked to respond to what I considered to be an ultimatum, I returned to the hostel intending to resign, but I was persuaded not to do so by Mrs Hawkins, the senior midwife. She said, "You have the option of three offers, so you do not have to accept this one. Tell her that you have no wish to go to the East End of London. After all, you are young, you ride a bicycle, the East End is near the docks, and it is a rough area. All the midwives who work there are married and drive cars."

I felt better for that advice, so I promptly phoned and repeated the words almost verbatim. The supervisor did not insist. Life continued at an even pace and I was enjoying working in the area, dodging in and out of the heavy traffic on the Holloway Road as if I had been a cyclist of long standing. Arsenal included some of the then-luxurious parts of Highbury, where a number of professionals, including doctors, up-and-coming celebrities, and writers, lived.

Once more my feeling of contentment was interrupted by another summons from the supervisor of midwives, with the offer of a transfer to an area in Hammersmith. Again I sought advice of the senior midwife, who said, "I know that area. The midwife is due to retire. She lives in a prefab building with her husband and children. The accommodation is next door to Wormwood Scrubs Prison. It is not the right place for you. Tell her you are not prepared to take that post."

She sat in the office whilst I made the phone call, and I got another reprieve. But the reprieve was short-lived for one Wednesday afternoon a fortnight later, I was offered a post in the Paddington and Marylebone District. When I told Mrs Hawkins of the Paddington and Marylebone offer, she said, "I don't know why she is offering you a post in that area. It comes under the Queen's Institute of District Nursing. It is different from the London County Council that employs you, and indeed all of us in North London. Their midwives are paid less than we are. She must have forgotten that. Remind her, and tell her that you wish to remain employed by the London County Council."

Once again, on Mrs Hawkins's advice I turned down the offer. The voice on the other end of the phone said, "Then find yourself another job!" I felt numb when I heard those words, for I realised that I had been dismissed from my post. My up to then willing advisor, distanced herself from the situation and offered no further support. I felt lost, alone, and concerned that I had no options left. I felt that I could not share these feelings with any of my colleagues.

By the weekend when, thankfully, I was off duty and away from the hostel, the feeling of helplessness had turned to one of fury, and I began to question her authority to dismiss me. After all, I thought, like me, she was only another employee of the London County Council. She was not at the interview. She had not appointed me.

On Sunday, still seething with fury, I wrote a letter to the Chief Medical Officer of Health at the London County Council outlining my concern and requesting that he gave the matter his personal attention. That done, I went back to the hostel later that evening in a calm and peaceful state of mind.

On the following Wednesday afternoon, an anxious and agitated superintendent greeted me when I returned to the hostel from the Antenatal Clinic. She asked, "Did you write to Dr Martin?"

Calmly, I replied, "Yes, I did."

"You didn't tell me."

"No, I didn't."

"Well, his secretary phoned with an appointment for you to see him. And the supervisor of midwives also phoned to ask what it was about."

"Oh, nothing really." Realising that I was not going to divulge any information, she retreated.

The following afternoon I kept my appointment with Dr Martin at his office. He was seated in a large and comfortable-looking armchair when his secretary ushered me in. I felt the measure of his eyes. I saw in them a glint of amusement when, in a soft indulgent tone of voice, he asked, "Are you Miss Allen?"

"Yes," I said.

He stood as I approached and, continuing in the same tone, he added, "You seem to have a lot to say for yourself."

I stopped, and averting my eyes to meet his, replied softly, but firmly. "If that's what you think, I had better not come any further."

He raised his eyebrows but retained an amused expression. Then, waving his arm in a half circular movement he indicated an armchair and said, "Oh, no. Do sit down, Miss Allen." Dr Martin said that he was unaware of the issues that I had raised in my letter. Over tea and biscuits he clarified the position by saying, "It is indeed correct that the Paddington and Marylebone District Midwifery service is provided by the Queens Institute of District Nursing. However, we will be taking over the service next year so, you see, your terms and condition of employment will remain unchanged. Does that make you feel differently about the offer?"

"Yes, it does, "I replied.

"Would you like to see what it is like at Paddington and Marylebone?"

"Yes, I'd love to."

"Then I will make the appointment for you to do so, and if you like what you see, I will arrange the transfer."

One morning the following week, I stood on the stairs leading to the building situated in a tree-lined Avenue in Maida Vale that served as the headquarters for the Paddington and Marylebone Queen's Nursing Service. I wondered what was awaiting me behind the heavy black door. I need not have worried, for as I was about to ring the bell, a dignified, medium-built person wearing a smile that was warmly welcoming opened the door.

"You must be Miss Allen. Do come in. We are expecting you. I am Miss Anderson, the superintendent. Did you find us easily?" she asked.

"Yes, I did. Thank you."

"Good," she said. Then she added, "I have asked our senior midwife to brief you and to show you around. You are invited to lunch with us. You will then have the opportunity to meet the other midwives. Later, you will join me for tea and a chat. Perhaps by then you will have made a decision, from what you have seen and heard, about whether you wish to come and join our team of midwives."

"Yes, thank you."

I was impressed with the tour of the building, the friendliness of the staff, and the different method of working. There was a team approach in the area that covered Paddington, Marylebone, and St John's Wood. I decided that this was the place where I wanted to work and told both Miss Anderson and Dr Martin.

The following month I became the sixth member of the team, with shared responsibility for the community midwifery service and the teaching and supervision of six student midwives. The area we covered extended from Notting Hill Gate in the south to Great Portland Street in the north. We took it in turn to be the "first midwife on call".

The Paddington, Bayswater, and Notting Hill areas were the busiest part of the district. They were also the least affluent. There were a number of tenement houses with a cold water tap on each floor where new arrivals from the West Indies, desperate for somewhere to live, were obliged to compromise their privacy and to share facilities with non-family members. There were also a number of Irish families in a similar predicament. Yet somehow they coped.

In those days there was a great stigma attached to being an unmarried mother. As district midwives we were often called out to frightened young women who were in labour and were living on their own in a tiny room. They would not have received any antenatal care, nor would they have made any preparation for their babies.

Therese was one such young girl, who was alone in a room on the ground floor of a large house in St Stephens Gardens. It was the screams from the room next door that had drawn the neighbour's attention. And on checking, she had found the terrified youngster. Her phone call came late one winter's evening. In an agitated voice she asked, "Is that the Midwife Headquarters?"

"Yes," I replied.

"There is a young girl in labour here in St Stephens Gardens. She is on her own. I am just the neighbour. I think the baby is coming. You must come now. She is in terrible pain."

"Who is her doctor?" I asked.

"She doesn't have a doctor. She is not a Londoner. She won't tell me where she comes from. She doesn't want her parents to know where she is. You can ask all the questions when you get here. You must come now!"

In those early days, mobile phones had not been invented. And as we could not always rely on the easy access to public telephones, we made sure before we left that one of our colleagues was aware of the address so that she could start the process of arranging for an emergency admission to the nearest maternity unit where there was a bed available.

With a student midwife in tow, we dashed off. The neighbour was a mature motherly woman, who had left the front door open for us whilst she stayed with the distressed young woman. The room felt damp from the cold. The only form of heating was a single-bar electric fire that the neighbour had brought in. Apart from a battered armchair and the single bed, there was no other furniture. A small Belling cooker stood on the floor in the corner but it needed mending. A large Thermos with tea was beside the bed. The lighting was a 40 watt bulb stuck in a socket in the high ceiling. The student midwife and I exchanged glances that acknowledged the hopelessness of the situation.

The terrified youngster held her neighbour's hand in a vice. Her teeth bit hard into a folded hand towel. Her big brown eyes looked pleadingly at us as we entered – begging for relief from her agony. We examined her. The baby's heart rate was strong and regular. Birth was not imminent. We gave her gas and air from the machine that we had brought with us, to ease her discomfort. And gently rubbing the base of her spine to help her to relax, I asked, "What's your name?"

"Therese," she replied.

"Therese, how old are you?"

"Sixteen," she replied.

"Do your parents know where you are?"

She shook her head.

"Would you like me to get in touch with them?"

With tears rolling down her cheek, she said, "They would kill me."

We remained silent for a while as I gathered my thoughts. Still rubbing her back, I asked, "Is there anyone else you would like me to get in touch with?"

She shook her head.

"That's okay," I said as reassuringly as I could. "Tell me, what would you like to happen to the baby when it is born?"

She replied, almost inaudibly, "He said I must give it away."

Once more we remained silent for a while. Then I asked, "Is that what you want to do?"

She nodded assent.

"That's fine," I said "Now I know what your wishes are; I will make sure that the midwives in the unit know. They will set the ball in motion for you. Don't worry, everything will be all right." There was an expression of relief on her face as she looked at me fully for the first time.

"Will you come with me?"

I wanted to say, "Yes, of course I will". But I was the midwife on call for that night, and there were likely to be calls from other women in labour.

"No, I won't be able to do so. I am so sorry. I am on call for the area, and I have to remain in the district to respond to them. Don't you worry; my colleague will be going with you. You will be in safe hands."

Her eyes turned pleadingly to the neighbour, who had been mopping her brow and stroking her hair throughout. The kindly woman smiled at her and said, "Don't you worry, love. I will come with you too."

At that moment, an ambulance with blue flashing lights arrived. The ambulance driver asked brusquely, "Where is the patient? Can she walk?"

"She is a youngster, and this is her first baby. She is terrified. She is in the early stage of labour, so be gentle with her," I replied.

"Are you coming with her?"

No, I am not, but her neighbour will, and so will my colleague."

"We are taking her to the Mothers Maternity Unit at Clapton in the East End. That is the nearest place that has a bed." Then he added, "We are very busy tonight."

I heaved a sigh of relief and said, "I am pleased that you are taking her there, for I know that she will be given the special support that she will need now and when the baby is born."

Somehow, my encounter with that frightened teenager, alone in a strange place and about to encounter a significant life-changing experience, brought back vivid memories of the day I arrived in England. That sudden feeling of loneliness, panic, and fear as I stood on the platform at Paddington Station amongst strangers and desperately hoping that a British Council Representative would come to my rescue.

Thankful that the neighbour was accompanying her and relieved that the unit to which she was being taken belonged to the Salvation Army, I made sure that she was as comfortable as possible for the journey. Then, stroking her face gently and concealing the lump that had arisen in my throat, I said goodbye.

Although many years have passed, I have found it difficult to erase the face of that young girl from my memory.

Workers at the Arrowroot factory

Children working in the Arrowroot field

Leaving Home 1958

Front Entrance of Essex County Hospital in 1958

The Nurses' Dining Room

Student Nurses studying

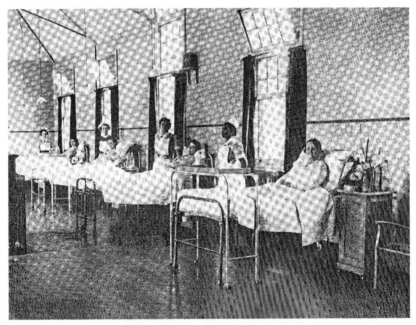

My first Ward at Myland hospital

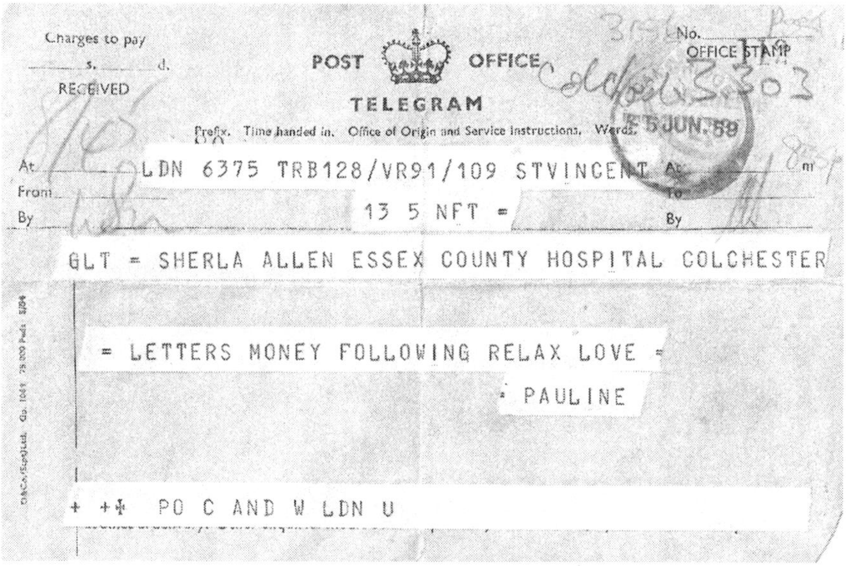
Charges to pay
s. d.
RECEIVED
POST OFFICE
TELEGRAM
Prefix. Time handed in. Office of Origin and Service Instructions. Words.
At LDN 6375 TRB128/VR91/109 STVINCENT
From 13 5 NFT =
By
GLT = SHERLA ALLEN ESSEX COUNTY HOSPITAL COLCHESTER
= LETTERS MONEY FOLLOWING RELAX LOVE =
= PAULINE
+ + PO C AND W LDN U

A Telegram from St Vincent

Newly Qualified Nurse

1978 Year of the Child Event at the Health Centre

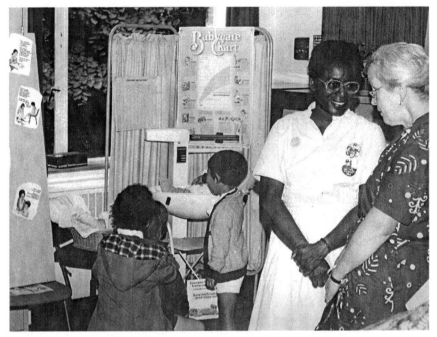

Open Day at the Health Clinic in 1978

Directors of SSAFA 1985

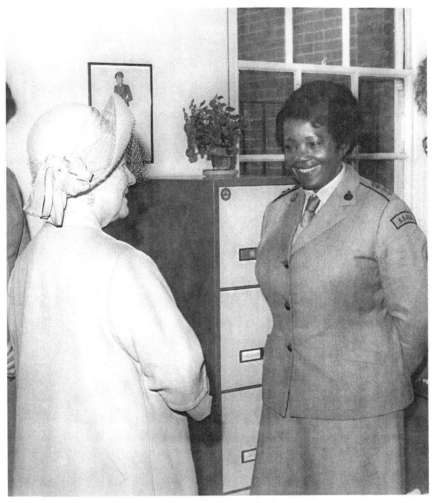

HRH The Queen Mother – Patron of SSAFA visiting in 1985

HRH Prince Michael of Kent President of SSAFA visiting in 1985

At HMS Tamar with Hong Kong Head of Service in 1985

Arriving by helicopter at the New Territories 1985

The Berliner train travelling through East Germany in 1985

Prime Minister meeting 50 Celebrated Women in the NHS - 1998

Colchester Nurses Reunion - PTS March 1958

Reunion Abbey Gardens - Bury St Edmunds 2008

Chapter 6:
Becoming a Nurse Manager

By the late 1960s there was a change in policy for the delivery of the maternity services. Those expectant mothers, whom we would normally have delivered in their own home, were now to be admitted routinely to hospital for their confinement. They were then to be discharged home after forty-eight hours, into the care of the community midwives. This meant that my role and responsibility as a community midwive would be reduced to that of a maternity nurse. It was a position I could not contemplate. I knew then that the time had come for me to move on.

Still nurturing a love affair with midwifery, I decided that my best course of action would be to accept the post of Night Sister in charge of a unit in North London. Somehow I did not find it easy to adapt to the hospital environment and its unsocial hours. I realised that I had made a grave mistake.

One night as I sat in the quiet room for my break, I was idly thumbing my way through a nursing journal when I saw an advertisement for suitably qualified and experienced British midwives. They were required to provide a midwifery service for the families of British Service men posted to Singapore.

Applicants were invited to apply to the head of nursing of an organisation called the Soldiers, Sailors, Airmen and Families Association (SSAFA). The idea of working overseas appealed to me. I had the appropriate nationality, qualification, and experience. I met the criteria, so I requested the application forms, completed and returned them, then waited for a response.

The reply that I received was not what I had expected. It was brief and to the point. It acknowledged that I had the relevant professional qualifications, however, as I was not British, I could not be considered for a post. Baffled by the reason that was given, I could hear somewhere far away a familiar voice ringing in my ears. It was Nurse Barton's voice, the student nurse from Colchester who had once said to me, "Don't say I didn't warn you."

Disappointed but undaunted, I remained in my post for a further six months, hoping that my disaffection with having to work in a hospital environment would resolve itself. But it did not. There were two questions I kept asking myself: What have I achieved? What are my prospects of climbing the professional nursing ladder?

The answers were stark: I was a qualified nurse and midwife. I now held the post of Night Sister in a small maternity unit after five years' post-graduate experience, and I felt trapped. My reaction to the feeling of being trapped was to return home. I had no idea what I was going to do when I got there, but the need to reconnect with my homeland was overwhelming. And so it was that in 1966, I made the journey.

I looked out of the window of the plane as it made its descent over the Caribbean Sea. The sun's rays were creating sparkles on the aquamarine waters. Memories of my childhood by the sea came floating back. I felt an emotional tug within my heart and the lifting of a weight from my shoulders – a weight that I must have acquired over the eight years of adjusting to living and working between two worlds. Home at last, it was easy to settle back into the leisurely atmosphere of the island, basking in the warmth of the sunshine and enjoying the sense of freedom.

There were noticeable improvements in the island and more opportunities for its people. Gone were the buses of the past that plied the country roads each morning on their way to the capital, carrying passengers, chickens, and the occasional goat. Now, there were overcrowded transit vans playing loud music and speeding recklessly along the narrow winding roads.

Revisiting old familiar places, I found that most of my friends had migrated to Canada under a special scheme agreed between the two Governments. Others had left to build new lives in the United States and England. The University of the West Indies that had its headquarters and main campus in Jamaica now had campuses in other islands. More of the young people were getting the opportunity to attend the University. There was an air of great optimism. And somehow I got caught up in the mood.

But I was disappointed to find that there were no suitable nursing posts. The suggestion of alternative employment in the Civil Service did not appeal to me. After an absence of eight years, little had changed in the island's health service. The old cottage-style colonial hospital based in the capital continued to be the main centre for health care. There were a number of small multi-purpose clinics where nurses provided a range of nursing and midwifery services to isolated villages. These services included forceps, twin, and breech deliveries. In the UK, such procedures were the responsibility of doctors, and I had no such skills.

Reluctantly, I had to accept that what the island had to offer would not be challenging enough for me. But I needed to have made the journey to come to that realization. I decided to return to London to develop my career within the Community Nursing Service. As this service was the responsibility of the Local Authority, it meant that I would have to apply to one of them for sponsorship to attend the course at the Queen's Institute of District Nursing.

The Institute was the only organisation approved to provide the training for registered nurses who wished to work in the community. The course was considered to be prestigious. Those who completed it successfully were known as Queen's Nurses and were held in high regard. I wanted to be one of those nurses. Also, I remembered from my past experience as a community midwife that I had more freedom to use my initiative than I did in the hospital environment.

———————————

Back in London, I was delighted to receive sponsorship to the course from the London Borough of Camden. Now I needed somewhere to live. So I was pleased to accept the offer of temporary accommodation at the nurses' home in Central London whilst I looked for a permanent place.

It was an advertisement that had appeared in the *Evening Standard* for a few days that eventually caught my attention. I telephoned the number that was quoted and a very cultured English male voice answered. "Yes," he said "The flat is still available."

"Can I come to view it now?" I asked.

"Yes, of course you can."

Remembering my discussion with the senior midwife at the maternity unit, I thought I ought to be forthright, so I added, "I need to tell you that I am from the West Indies. Does that make a difference?"

"Good God, what does that matter?" was the response.

Excited, I hailed a taxi and went to view the accommodation. It was situated in Hampstead Lane. I realised when I got there that it was the part of Highgate Village, where the well-heeled lived. Yes, the rental would be greater than I had budgeted, but be that as it may, I made up my mind as I walked towards the front door that I would take the flat and deal with the matter of payment later.

The property was a large, imposing, three-storied detached house. It was owned by two brothers. One was a farmer in Yorkshire, and the other an international lawyer. He occupied the upper floor. An elderly English couple had the middle floor, and I, the ground. Apart from the requirement to pay a weekly rental of £12.00, there were no restrictions. I thought, as I said goodbye to my new landlord and surveyed the area whilst I waited for the bus, Dear Hampstead Lane, a penniless nurse is about to enter your world.

I felt that I had arrived at another planet when I moved to my new neighbourhood. The residents, mainly professionals, were polite, interested but not intrusive. I wondered how it was possible for two parts of the same city to be so different. The experience of living in that part of North London was in great contrast to that of living in the East End. I had continued to maintain a reserve but that proved not to be necessary. There was a greater generosity of spirit in this community.

This was the time of the Vietnam War. The brother of one of my neighbours was a journalist and reporter in the war zone. There were many evenings when the war was the subject of lengthy discussions. They invited me into their world, and I in turn invited them into mine.

I lived next door to Joseph and Marina, a couple who were of German origin. Marina was an artist and potter. Together they ran a successful nationwide pottery business. I was on nodding acquaintance with both of them. This was the situation for approximately six months when, on exchanging my usual "Nice day" greeting with Marina, she said "I think we have gone beyond that polite greeting of the English. Come in for a drink."

"Thank you," I said as I entered her house.

"We did not drink tea then, nor did we on any other occasion."

That was to be the first of many social encounters and the beginning of a thirty-year friendship that continues today with the younger members of her family.

In the 1960s, the notion of providing a nursing service to patients in their own homes was not generally understood by some of the nurses who opted for a career in hospital. They believed that those of us who worked in the community, were not as qualified and experienced as they were. They had come to that conclusion because, unlike them, we were not employed by the NHS, but by the Queen's Institute of District Nursing and later, by the London Borough of Camden.

Camden's boundary extended from Highgate and Hampstead in the North to Covent Gardens and Leicester Square in the South, and I was eager to join the group of Queen's nurses who provided the service to the residents living in the south. This part of the Borough seemed more vibrant and had the greatest cultural and social mix. We often referred to the residents who lived in the Bloomsbury area as the "intellectuals". There were also actors, artists, and cockneys living alongside older, long-standing English tenants in low-cost accommodation that belonged to the Peabody Trust.

Covent Garden, at that time, had a flourishing fruit, vegetable, and flower market during the day. But at night it became a glittering Theatre Land. In those days, well-dressed individuals on their way to concerts or plays could occasionally be seen doing a dainty jig to avoid a rat as it scurried across the pavement, having dined on the scraps left behind by the market stalls vendors. Today, that area is much improved and gentrified, although people attending concerts and plays no longer dress so elegantly.

I spent a fortnight in Rye in Sussex, as part of my Queen's Nurses' training. I stayed with Miss Parker, who worked as the nurse, the district midwife, and the health visitor. She was expected to divide her time between the roles, but priority had to be given to the mother in labour. It was customary for nurses in rural areas to have these three nursing duties. They were provided with accommodation and transport.

A car was the usual means of transport. It was easily identifiable as the name of the County was engraved on both doors.

On my first evening in Rye, Miss Parker sat beside the fireplace and unfolded a number of large sheets of newspaper. These she made into what appeared to me to be paper boats.

"Are those boats for the children to play with at the clinic?" I asked.

She smiled as she said, "I was expecting that question. These are not boats. They are paper bins for me to dispose of dressings when I visit the patients. In hospital, there are bins for that purpose. Here on the district, we have to improvise." This was in the days before the advent of plastic bags.

It was whilst I was there that I began to understand what it would mean to be a Queen's Nurse. I realised that it was much more than giving nursing care. I noticed that the relationship between Miss Parker and her patients was friendly but professional. She sought their views and took them into account. I liked the approach and thought, how different this is from what happened in the hospitals. There, it was accepted practice for us to see the patient through the eyes of the illness, to take control, and to concentrate on curing the condition often without the involvement of the patient.

On the second morning that I visited with Miss Parker, one of her patients welcomed us with a beaming smile and the words "Nurse, thank you for the wheelchair and for getting the ramp fitted. The workmen came yesterday afternoon. And, the optician also called to test my eyes."

"Why did the patient thank you for the ramp and wheelchair?" I asked as we left the house and walked towards the car. Miss Parker gave me a quizzical glance before she replied, "This patient we have just visited was referred to me last week. She is a diabetic with failing vision and is unsteady on her legs. All that I have been asked to do is to give her a daily insulin injection."

As I continued to look puzzled, she said, "You heard her thanking me for the wheelchair and the ramp. You also heard her say that the optician had visited?"

"Yes," I replied.

"I ordered those services. She is now able to see. Her niece can wheel her out into the garden and to the shops. That is what I mean when I say it is not enough just to perform the basic nursing care. We must also look at the whole person and consider what would improve the quality of life." I nodded, made a mental note, and have tried to adopt that approach in my work ever since.

I had been staying with Miss Parker for five days, and I had got into a daily routine. But on the sixth morning, when I woke, my hostess was not there. She had pinned a note on the bedroom door. It read, "Early-morning call to a mother in labour at one of the farms. Not sure how long it will take. Help yourself to breakfast."

I had just finished having my breakfast when Miss Parker returned and joined me at the table. She explained, "We will be doing a return visit to the mother and baby later today. The family are Travellers."

"Travellers?" I asked

"Some people call them Gypsies. They live in mobile homes or caravans and tend to travel around the country. They usually come here at this time of year to pick the apples and strawberries at the farms."

"Why did they come to pick fruits knowing that the baby was due?"

"The baby was not due for another four weeks, so she wasn't expecting to go into labour so soon. Anyway she now has a lovely little boy and seems happy enough."

Later, when we made the return visit to the new baby and his mother; I was able to appreciate further what was entailed in the work of a nurse who undertook triple duties. Miss Parker was alert to the risk of cross-infection. She washed her hands carefully and often. She kept her midwifery equipment and uniforms separately – an approach that today's health professionals may wish to consider.

The 1960s was an ideal time for me to be part of a district nursing service that was managed by the London Borough of Camden. The Borough's medical officer was responsible for the provision of the health and social services – including housing and education. He was well-known for his commitment to improve the health of the residents of Camden. This made it easier for the Queen's Nurses to offer a coordinated and seamless service that met the needs of their patients.

But by the early 1970s, there were signs that the seamless service was about to lose its impact. There was a rumour that the Government was planning to reorganise the NHS and to transfer the community health aspect. The social care services would remain the Borough's responsibility. I did not understand the reason for the decision, and instinctively I felt that a career change was looming.

Thirty years later, the policy of separation of the health and social care services remains. The present arrangements for the delivery of health and social care have further cemented the divide. Both organisations are funded and managed separately. They are expected to collaborate and to provide a service similar to that of the 1960s. But there is a lack of agreement as to what constitutes health and what is considered to be social care. Whilst this uncertainty continues, district nurses and their patients are caught in a quandary, and the desire for a seamless service is unlikely to be achieved.

It was the beginning of my fourth year as a Queen's Nurse, and I was becoming restless. I knew that it was time for me to move on, but once again I was not sure what I wanted to do or where I wanted to go.

A New Year's Eve party in 1970 and a chance meeting with Barbara gave me the spur to act. We had attended the same school at home, but I had not seen her since we both came to England to undertake the training to become qualified nurses. We had a great deal to talk about – including our careers. She was being sponsored for the Health Visitors course at one of the polytechnics.

"It is different from nursing," she said with enthusiasm. "It combines education with training. The tutors encourage you to think – They don't spoon-feed you as they do in nurses' training schools. They encourage you to debate, to research, and to present your views logically. You meet other non-nursing students. I feel as if I've got new brain cells."

I began to get excited and asked, "What do you have to do to get on the course?"

"Two things," she replied. "But they have to be done together. You must apply to a Borough for sponsorship and to a polytechnic for a place on the course. The polytechnic will not accept you unless you have proof of sponsorship. The adverts are now in the nursing journals. You will have to apply to more than one to have a greater chance of success."

"When does the course start?" I asked

"It begins at the end of September. You have got to start applying now, otherwise it will be too late for this year."

I felt as if I had received a new burst of energy. The New Year suddenly had a brighter hue. I left the party elated and enthused, determined to develop a career in health visiting. I applied for the course and was successful in getting sponsorship from the London Borough of Waltham Forest. At the end of September, I joined thirty-five other health visitor students at a polytechnic in the East End of London.

Driving daily from Highgate in North London to the East End was not an easy journey. But this was only one of many difficulties I had to overcome. I had not done any studying during the past four years. I knew nothing about research methods. As a student health visitor, I was expected to present papers to my peers in the seminar groups and to respond to their questions and challenges. I can still remember vividly the grilling they gave me when I presented a paper on "poverty".

It was on this occasion that I woke up to the realization that the concept of poverty for people from the Caribbean was different from the concept of those who are from the United Kingdom. I had stated that anyone who owned a television could not be considered to be poor. The members of the group disagreed vehemently with me. They put forward convincing reasons why a television was no longer a luxury. From the lively debate that followed and the consensus that was reached, I realised once again that I had been living between two worlds.

While I was adjusting to the liberating feeling of student life, I was also committed to the four principles of health visiting. These principles included the search for health needs, the stimulation of the awareness of those needs, the importance of influencing policies that affect health, and the need to facilitate health-enhancing activities. These principles affected the way I would see the world around me in the future.

The academic year came to an end in September, and I was now a qualified health visitor ready for full-time employment in the Borough of Waltham Forest. The Borough, which was once part of the County of Essex, has borders with Redbridge, Newham, Enfield, Haringey, and Hackney. Epping Forest was not far away.

I joined two experienced health visitors and shared the office with them at a clinic in Leyton – the southernmost part of the Borough, which bordered with Hackney. They were kind and helpful. Looking back, I believe that I must have exhausted them with my eagerness to change the world. They often teased me whenever I became too enthusiastic by saying that I had "caught religion".

I became the health visitor responsible for families that lived around the southern end of the Lee field Road close to a local football ground. The area had its share of elderly widows who had lived there for the greater part of their lives. Some were housebound. As time went by, a number of young couples moved from Hackney to start their married lives, having bought maisonettes on what was a private estate.

Before long, the new arrivals began to have their own families and attended a clinic that I held in a local church hall. We had a special place for the toddlers to play. In such a relaxed atmosphere, it was easy for me to observe the children's developmental progress and the interaction of their mothers. It was also an opportunity for the families to learn from one another and to form a support group. It is surprising how quickly the helpless baby grows into a cruising toddler exploring the space around. Soon a maisonette becomes too confined, and a bigger and safer place has to be found.

Health visitors at that time had a responsibility for registering daily minders, liaising with the nurseries, playgroups, and mother and toddler groups in their area. I felt that I had found a solution. The local football facility was close by. It was not being used during the day. One morning, I paid a visit to see the person who was responsible for the premises.

A pleasant middle-aged man was sitting on a chair having a cup of tea. He looked surprised but greeted me by saying, "What can I do for you, love?"

"Good morning," I said with a smile. "I am one of the nurses from the clinic, and I've come to ask a favour."

He rose from the chair still holding his mug. "Would you like a cup? I've just made this one. The kettle is still hot."

"Yes please," I said, for I wanted to see the inside of the premises. I followed him. The place was well kept and had what we needed. As I sat to have my cup of tea, I asked, "Do you use this building every day?"

"We do on some evenings and on weekends," he replied.

"There are a number of young couples with toddlers who have recently moved into the area. They live on the private estate. One of them was a primary school teacher. We were wondering if the members of the club would allow us to hold a mother and toddler group here on one afternoon each week."

He replied by saying, "I notice some young people with prams and push chairs in the roads along here recently."

"Yes," I replied. "Most of them are new to the area, and it will be a good way for them to get to know one another and for the children to play together."

"I can appreciate that," he said. "But I don't know what the powers that be would say. I will put it to them and I will let you know. Mind you, I am not making any promises."

"When would you be able to give me an answer?" I asked

"Give me a fortnight. I am here every day at this time, so drop in."

"Thank you very much," I said and left feeling somewhat hopeful.

Two weeks later we were given permission. On reflection, I do not believe that in today's climate we would have been allowed to use the premises, because of the strict health and safety regulations.

As I attempted to apply the four health visiting principles to my everyday practice, I began to observe more critically the neighbourhoods where the families lived. I now looked for what was healthy about them and what was not. And I asked myself, What can a health visitor do to make a positive difference?

I recall a visit I paid in my early days to a family who was living in a house on one of the council estates. The children were prone to breathing problems and were often absent from school. As I entered the house, there was a strong smell of dry-cleaning fluid. It was so strong that I began to cough uncontrollably.

"Everybody coughs like that when they come here," the mother said as she welcomed me into her home.

"Do you know why?" I asked.

"I think it is because the house backs on to a laundry and dry-cleaning place, and we get the fumes. It is not so bad on a Sunday or Bank holidays."

"Have you asked the environmental health officer to visit you?"

"No," she replied.

"Would you like me to request a visit?"

"No! No! You see this is the only four-bedroomed house on the estate, and we don't want to move to a tower block."

I could not persuade her to change her mind. But I was uneasy about the family's health problems and felt that I needed to act. I was also wrestling with a quotation from Florence Nightingale that was recorded in the publication "Health Visiting Principles in Practice". Florence wrote, in 1891, "The needs of home health bringing require different qualifications [from that of nursing the sick]; she [the health visitor] will require tact and judgement unlimited lest the work be regarded as interference and become unpopular."

In the end I decided to influence policy by expressing my concerns to the Environmental Health Department about the strong fumes that appeared to be coming from the dry-cleaning establishment. I asked them to pay a visit. They did. And a few months later, the business was relocated elsewhere and away from the council estate.

Some may consider my intervention to be interference. But I would argue that this was simply an example of good health visiting practice, as I had successfully applied one of the key principles of health visiting, the need to influence policy, to bring about an improvement in this family's health.

In 1975, there was a major change in the delivery of health visiting services. In the past health visitors had the responsibility for families living in defined geographical areas. This was altered in preference to an arrangement where health visitors were to be responsible for families that were registered with general practitioners. This was the first step towards what was later to become known as "GP Attachment".

It was not as simple an adjustment to make as we were led to believe. Nor was it easy to explain to families with whom we had worked, that we were no longer their health visitor. It also meant that on occasions three or four health visitors could be seen visiting families in the same road. I was never sure whether this restructuring led to a waste of scarce resources or an improvement in the quality of the service.

I had been working with the new system for some months and was getting to know the families who were registered with the doctors in the practice. I had even succeeded in establishing a trusting relationship with the doctors and was invited to their weekly management meetings. It was at one of these meetings that I introduced the topic of a confidential counselling service for young couples who were finding it difficult to adjust to life with their newborn babies. As there was no enthusiasm for the suggestion, I did not pursue it.

One morning I was sitting at my desk in the clinic when the telephone rang, and the voice at the other end of the line said, "Good morning. May I speak to the health visitor for the Lee field Road area?"

"Speaking," I replied.

"I am the Chairman of the local Marriage Guidance Council. We would like to invite you as one of our guests to a cheese and wine party we are having next Friday evening. Are you able to come? "

"Oh!" I said trying not to sound surprised. "I would love to." I replaced the receiver and, turning to my two colleagues, I said, "Guess what that phone call was about."

They stared at me blankly.

"I have just been invited by none other than the Chairman of the local Marriage Guidance Council to a cheese and wine party."

"What?" they exclaimed in unison. "How did you manage that?"

"I don't know. But no doubt I shall find out next Friday."

I was surprised to be greeted by one of the female doctors from the practice when I arrived at the party. "I didn't know that you were going to be here," I said as I took off my coat.

"Let me introduce you to the Chairman," she said.

"Do you know him?" I asked.

"Yes, I do. He is my husband. When I heard you raise the question of counselling at the meeting the other day, I thought I would tell him about your suggestion."

"I was not thinking of sending the patients to marriage guidance," I replied. "I was thinking of offering a service at the practice."

"I realise that. But counsellors need to be trained if they are to be effective in what they do." Taking hold of my hand, she led me in the direction of her husband and said," This is the health visitor who is interested in counselling."

Before long I was having a chat with the Chairman in his office; I learnt what was entailed in the training to become a counsellor. And although that was not something I had thought of pursuing, by the end of the evening I had agreed to be put forward for selection.

This was 1975. The training took place on weekends over a period of approximately two years at the National Headquarters in Rugby. I did not know what to expect. But at the end of each of the weekends that I spent at the college in Rugby, I returned to work at the clinic with a broader perspective of life. This increased awareness also brought a different dimension to my health visiting practice. I was able to pick up subtle cues about relationships within families that I visited and to offer a level of support and guidance that I could not have done in the past.

One afternoon I returned from the clinic at the church hall to find a note on my desk, asking me to make an appointment to see the Chief Nurse of the Community Nursing Service. Waving the note at my colleagues I asked, "Do you know what this is about?"

"We think it is to offer to send you on the management training course. They have offered it to us but we have refused. It is a waste of our nursing skills. All the managers seem to do is to shuffle paper around and attend meetings."

I made an appointment to see her later that week. The interview was professional but friendly. She asked, "How long have you been working with us?"

"Almost five years," I replied.

"Are you still enjoying the work?"

"Oh yes, very much so."

"Have you any plans for developing your career further?"

"Yes," I said and added, "I was going to ask if you would consider seconding me to do the Diploma in Health Education next year I believe it would help to improve the planning and presentation of the health promotion sessions that I have been doing at the clinic."

"I am afraid we won't be able to do that from our nursing budget; the Health Education Department is responsible for the sponsorship of students for the Diploma course."

I was disappointed and remained quiet for a while.

"The reason I have asked you to come to see me is to offer you the opportunity to attend the First Line Management course. Would you be interested in doing that?"

"Does that mean that I would have to apply for a management post once I have done the course?" I asked

"No it does not. It is intended to give nurses an insight into ways of managing their work more effectively. If in the end you decide to become a manager that would be a by-product."

I decided to accept the offer of the management course much to the disapproval of my two colleagues.

Chapter 7:
Managing Community Nurses

It was at one of our monthly Health Visitor staff meetings that a colleague from one of the other clinics passed a clipping to me. The clipping was from a nursing journal.

"I think that you can do this job," she wrote. "It is in North London where you live. The closing date is at the end of the week."

The clipping was an advertisement for a nursing officer with district nursing and health visiting experience. The nursing officer would manage district nurses, who provided a nursing service in the community. The post holder would also be responsible for the management of specialist family health visitors who promoted health in the community, and who monitored the development of children to ensure that the needs of the families were met.

The post would involve working together with other professionals and organisations to improve the health and well-being of residents in Hampstead and Belsize Park.

I had not seen this advert and had no plans to change my job. But I was grateful for the suggestion as a change would enable me to work closer to home. And as it was also eighteen months since I had completed the First Line Management course I felt that this was an opportunity to gain practical management experience. I decided to apply for this post. I realised that I had limited time in which to submit an application; I telephoned the person in charge to ask for an informal interview.

The following afternoon I was sitting in her office where she described the changes that were occurring in the Hampstead District. She said, "We have got a new Divisional Nursing Officer, who is making changes. We have members of staff that have been here for many years and in that respect we have a stable workforce. They will be expected to adapt to these changes."

I asked her if this was a newly created post. She replied, "No, it is not a new one. The previous post-holder has retired after twenty-eight years. In the days when she was appointed, the post was limited to that of a Clinic Superintendent. Today we are called Nursing Officers and our role is much wider."

I understood what she meant. Nursing officers were responsible for managing and developing community services; this was different from the role of clinic superintendents. "How large is the geographical area?" I enquired

"It is not very large. Some of the health visitors walk to do their visits. The area extends from Finchley Road to Hampstead Heath. There are two health clinics. One is in Hampstead Village and the other is in Belsize Park."

I thought that it would not be worth pursuing the application for the post if there were a preferred internal candidate, so I asked, "Has anyone from within the district applied for the post?"

"One of the members of staff has applied. She has been doing the work on a temporary basis. You should not allow that to put you off applying. I would encourage you to submit an application."

"I do not have the forms, and the closing date is on Friday."

"That can be easily resolved" she said, and she turned to dial a number and ask for the forms to be brought to her office. I completed the forms in one of the vacant offices, delivered it by hand to the Personnel department, and returned to work the next day, not daring to tell my colleagues what I had done.

I had felt encouraged by this meeting. I had the experience of having worked as a district nurse and a health visitor. Her decision to let me complete the application and hand it directly to her personnel department made me feel hopeful.

I was short-listed for the interview and offered the post. In hindsight, I believe that the Divisional Nursing Officer was looking to appoint an applicant from outside of the district, one who would bring a different perspective and new ideas to the post.

As the final days of my work in Waltham Forest were coming to an end, I felt a heaviness of heart. I had not only enjoyed working with my two colleagues, but we had, over the five years, become firm friends. Now I was about to venture into the unknown world of community health service management, in a place where it seemed to me that the staff had become permanent fixtures. And I was getting anxious.

The year was 1977 and at the beginning of May, I arrived at my new office, where I was greeted warmly by the health visitor who had also applied for the post and had worked as the Acting Manager. She was given the responsibility of introducing me to the members of staff, who were polite but guarded. I felt that this must be an uncomfortable situation as I had been offered the post that she wanted. And I wondered how she really felt about my appointment

My office was located in a prefabricated building that served as a family health clinic and specialist play group. There was another clinic that was housed in the basement of a block of Council flats in Hampstead Village.

I was responsible for managing two teams of school nurses and family health visitors and a specialist team of health visitors who worked with the elderly. The teams seemed to work well together. They had enjoyed an easy relationship with my predecessor and administrative staff. They had no difficulty in getting the resources that they needed. As far as they were concerned, I was going to interfere and they would have preferred to have had an insider appointed to the post.

One Tuesday morning I was walking towards the entrance of the clinic in Hampstead Village. Someone whom I had not met was doing likewise. At the door, she turned to me and said, "I hope you are not going to interfere with the way that my health visitors do their work. This is a very middle-class area. The families here are intelligent and do not need to be visited routinely by them."

Inwardly seething, I thought, They are not your health visitors.

"I am not going to interfere with your health visitors. I am here to see the health visitors employed by the Hampstead Health Authority," I replied with a smile.

She adjusted her handbag, extended her arm and introduced herself as the doctor responsible for running the local baby clinic. From that encounter, I realised that the health visitors had sought allies who would support them in resisting any possible changes that I might wish to make as their manager. I thought to myself, "This is going to be an interesting experience."

The new Divisional Nursing Officer intended to make changes to the way the community health services were organised and delivered. The District had been slower than Waltham Forest in changing from working within defined geographical boundaries to the system of GP Attachment. Health visitors would need to make links with GPs and those members of staff who preferred to work within geographical boundaries would be expected to adapt to new ways of working.

Most of the health visitors were not in favour of the change. And as the GPs had their practices in private property we could not alter the way they chose to work. GPs were not employees of the Community Health Service. This meant that successful GP Attachments were difficult to secure. I decided that a new approach to this challenge was required. As we could not force them to change, we could try to encourage them.

1978 was the Year of the Child. I felt that this presented us with an unique opportunity to draw the wider community's attention to the health services that we provided. So I suggested to the members of staff that we hold an "Open Day" at the clinic in the Belsize area, where members of the public, teachers, and school children, including those from the private schools could mingle with the staff. We announced the activity on a local radio station.

The Open Day was well received. Several local GPs attended, and so did many of the wealthier middle-class families. These were the families that I was told did not need intensive health visiting. They were relaxed and seemed to benefit from the event. Local teachers who attended were keen to draw on our expertise. One result was that our health visitors were invited to advise some of the schools with their Health Education programmes.

The event also made more people aware of the services that we provided, and they began to use them. We were particularly pleased to see that teenage boys felt that they could drift into the clinic to seek advice without embarrassment. We had a lot of fun organising and running this event, and it changed our relationship with the local GPs. They began to ask us what they needed to do to get one of our health visitors to become attached to their practice. This was much to the surprise of those members of staff who preferred to work within geographical boundaries. Even the practice that was most resistant to our offer of this service phoned to enquire and to arrange an appointment. This was a long-established family practice. Their list of registered patients was smaller and more selective than others. They had the largest number of the affluent middle-class patients.

The following week I met with the doctors. I received a very warm welcome. Previously they had been polite, but frosty. Then one of the doctors asked, "Is the offer of the health visitors still available to us?"

"Yes," I replied.

"I read about the event you had at your clinic recently. I was told that it was a success. We would like one of your health visitors to be attached to our practice."

"Can I ask what has made you change your mind?"

They exchanged glances before answering the question. "Our senior partner will be retiring at the end of the year. We are planning to expand this practice and the services that we offer. We would like to include health visiting in the expanded services. We will be applying for "change of use" for the premises.

The need for some GPs to apply for change of use for the premises had delayed the attachment of health visitors to their practices. It was good news that this particular group of GPs were prepared to make the change. I hoped it would encourage others to do likewise. I was amazed but pleased that I was about to achieve what I had been told would be impossible.

"Are you intending to have another partner in the practice?"

"Yes. We have someone who is keen to join us. He has an interest in child health and is used to working with health visitors. Can we rely on your support for our application for change of use?"

"I will advise the Chief Nursing Officer of your plans. The decision rests with her," I replied.

The Chief Nursing Officer supported the application for the change of use, and two health visitors were relocated to the practice. Often people are more ready for change than we think. I have found that by experimenting with something new and meeting people halfway, they can adapt to change. This was the beginning of the successful acceptance of GP attachment in the district. A fun and well-organised event had helped to overcome long-standing obstacles and to bring opportunities to change.

1979 was the winter of discontent. It was a strange year. The dustbins were not being emptied; rats were taking over the streets. The fire engines changed colour from red to green as the Army had become responsible for the delivery of fire services. There was a feeling that things were going to change dramatically. Even the impossible thought of a woman leading this country was about to become a distinct possibility. A general election took place that year and with it came a change of government. There was speculation that the NHS was one of the organisations that was going to undergo a radical restructure.

During that year, I was enjoying the work I was doing in developing the Hampstead Community Health Service. The community staff had grown accustomed to having me as their manager and we were working well together. Together we had brought in a number of changes to the way they worked. We had extended our family planning clinics. We had even offered a room to a marriage guidance counsellor for one afternoon each week. The experience I had in Waltham Forest with the Marriage Guidance Council proved to be useful.

We offered the use of our clinic to one of the group practices to hold child health sessions for the families that were registered with them. We established a nurse-led school health service, and the links we had made within the community continued to expand. We began to deliver an holistic service that looked at the whole person, the family, and their needs.

I was doing a job that I liked in the way that I liked. This was the most pleasant experience of my nursing career to date. I worked with genuinely good people who had a lot of character, fire, spirit, and personal commitment to the development of community health services.

That was all about to change. In 1982 it became official. The NHS was about to be restructured. It seemed that more emphasis was going to be placed on treatment within a hospital setting. I felt that the initials NHS would no longer mean National Health Service, but rather it was about to become a National Hospital Service.

Most of the work that we were doing to keep people well and healthy, invaluable work that could not be measured easily, was likely to cease. More money was going to be spent on fixing sick people. An effective community health service saves money and improves quality of life in the long term. But we were about to be denied the opportunity to prove this.

I really did not imagine that this reorganisation of the NHS would be as radical as the one carried out in 1974, but I was wrong. The Government had identified mismanagement and maladministration as malaise within the NHS. Early in 1983, a team led by Sir Roy Griffiths, director of Sainsbury, undertook an inquiry into the effective use of manpower and related resources in the NHS. The inquiry recommended changes to the way in which the organisation would be managed in the future. One of the recommendations was the creation and introduction of a new general management structure.

Professional managers were recruited from outside and inside the organisation. This would be a departure from management by consensus led by health practitioners that was the custom at that time. The new managers were going to have more say in the allocation of resources than the clinicians. Today, the cost of management and administration is a sizeable part of the NHS budget. This was not the situation prior to 1983.

I was not ready for a change of post for I was enjoying the challenge and the opportunity to work with a team of enthusiastic health professionals. But the Griffiths recommendations were accepted and the winds of change blew strongly. The year was going to bring to a halt our development plans. Those who held senior management positions were told to apply for a post within the new structure. Many of my colleagues and line managers who were in post when I was appointed were offered a redundancy package. Others opted for early retirement.

It was the first time in the history of the NHS that a competitive rather than a collaborative element was to be introduced. And there was no guarantee that any of the current managers would be reappointed. Initially, the nursing officer grade was not required to reapply for their posts. . We felt insecure as we did not know how long this would remain the case.

It was at this point that an advertisement in one of the nursing journals attracted my attention. "Suitably qualified nurse managers in the NHS, who have a health visiting background, are invited to apply for a two-year contract to become the Professional head of the Soldiers Sailors, Airmen and Families Association Overseas Nursing Service."

I thought, With a two year contract, I will be able to escape the upheaval in the NHS and reapply for a post once things have settled. More than twenty years later, things still have not settled. In retrospect, I was naive to have entertained that thought.

I felt that I now needed to gain a broader experience as a manager and I believed that the international element that the post offered would provide that opportunity. So I requested an information pack and application forms.

The response came within a few days. On opening the envelope I realised that this was the same organisation the Soldiers, Sailors, Airmen and Families Association that had turned down my application to join their overseas midwifery service in the 1960s. At the time I had been rejected on the grounds that I was not considered to be a British subject.

I felt certain that things had changed by the 1980s, but just as a precaution to ensure that they had changed, I asked for an informal interview with the SSAFA Head of Service. I visited her at her office in Queen Anne's Gate, near St James's Park. It was in an imposing four-storied building that had kept its original features. I rang the bell, and the door was opened by a janitor in military-style uniform. He welcomed me politely and escorted me to the waiting room. It felt more like the home of a wealthy person rather than an organisation's office. It was certainly unlike the NHS prefabricated building where I had my office.

Going for an informal interview turned out to be worthwhile. The Head of the service was a charming English woman with a military bearing. She had spent her nursing and health visiting career working with the Armed Forces. She had served the Army as a Queen Alexandra Nurse and worked with the SSAFA Overseas Nursing Service as a health visitor.

She stood as I entered her office. "It is good of you to take the time to come for an informal chat. Let me take your coat. I have set aside an hour and will do my best to inform you of the work we do in SSAFA. Do have a seat." She looked at her watch and then said, "Coffee is usually brought to my office at this time. Would you prefer tea?"

"Coffee will be fine, thank you," I replied.

At ten o'clock promptly, there was a tap on the door of her office. "Come in," she said. "That will be my secretary, Miss Marks"

A smartly dressed middle-aged woman entered, carrying a tray laid with delicate bone china ware and homemade cookies. She placed the tray on a table, poured the coffee, and served us. I realised that I was entering another world, with a very different culture to that of the NHS, and that fine manners, good conduct, and politeness were an important part of their way of working.

"Thank you Miss Marks," said her boss, nodding stiffly. "I will not be accepting any calls for the next hour. Please display the engaged sign when you close the door." With a smile, she turned to me and asked, "Where shall we start? How much do you know about the Soldiers, Sailors, Airmen and Families Association? Are you aware that as well as its Nursing and Social Work services, there is a welfare arm that offers support to former servicemen and women?"

"I know absolutely nothing about the organisation – hence the reason for this visit." I sat back and began to learn about the history, values, unique culture, and terminology of the organisation. As she continued, I really felt that I was being taken on a journey into another world.

"SSAFA, the organisation, will be celebrating its centenary in February 1985 – two years hence. We have already begun to plan a year long celebration of activities throughout the various overseas Commands."

"Does that mean that the SSAFA Nursing Service will be one hundred years old also?" I asked.

"No," she replied. "The Nursing Service will celebrate its centenary in 1992. And I dare say that if you were successful in being appointed to the post, you will be very involved in planning and organising those events with the SSAFA Sisters."

"SSAFA Sisters?" I repeated

"Oh," she replied. "This is a friendly term that our military colleagues use whenever they refer to our health visitors."

Somewhat puzzled by the words "Overseas Commands", I asked, "These Commands that you refer to, what and where are they?"

"This is the term we use to refer to those places where there is a significant British military presence." Then she added, "I think you will gain a clearer picture and a better understanding of SSAFA's role if I were to point things out to you on the map." With that she rose from her chair and walked to the far end of the office, where there were several maps.

I tried to absorb as much as I could in this short informal interview. I learnt as she pointed to the various countries, that the largest Command was in Germany and was known as British Forces Germany (BFG). This stretched from Mönchengladbach in the south to beyond Hohne in the north. Berlin was managed separately. BFG also had special arrangements to provide a service for some NATO personnel serving in Afcent Liege and Maastricht.

The other Commands, although smaller, were of great strategic importance to the military. These, which she referred to as far-flung, included Gibraltar, Cyprus, and Hong Kong. The SSAFA Sisters in Hong Kong were expected to provide a service to the small number of British families serving with the Brigade of Gurkhas, in Brunei.

I had heard of the Gurkhas. They were renowned for their bravery and ability as soldiers. I remembered that they had formed part of the personal bodyguard for Queen Victoria in the nineteenth century, and they were still performing this role at certain ceremonial functions.

Not yet disconnected from an NHS view of the world, I asked, "Are there any specific health reasons for the strategic importance of these far-flung places?"

She replied by saying, "Let us return to our seats and I shall explain. In 1948, when the NHS was established, SSAFA was contracted by the Ministry of Defence to provide a community nursing service for the families of servicemen and women serving with the three Armed Forces overseas. The strategic importance relates to a military imperative – not to SSAFA and its nursing service."

The fog that had existed in my brain when I arrived gradually lifted as she continued to describe the organisation and its work. I found myself becoming fascinated by the organisation and the scale of its operation. I felt that this was going to give me an excellent opportunity to develop and to demonstrate my management skills. I was also beginning to learn about the difference between military personnel and the vast array of civilians that help them to perform their duties. "In the case of an outbreak of war, what will be the role of the SSAFA Sisters?" I asked.

She responded, "Members of staff who are posted to an overseas Command remain civilians throughout their stay in the service. They are there to look after the families. They are referred to as 'Civilians attached'. Although we are civilians, our contractual agreement with the MoD requires us to operate under military law. We are not always privy to these laws, but we are nonetheless required to adhere strictly to them."

She must have noticed that my glazed expression had disappeared for she gave a reassuring smile as she said, "There, you see, it is not as complicated as you imagined it to be. I have told you a great deal that is difficult to assimilate in an hour." She retrieved a file from the drawer of her desk and handing it to me, she continued, "In this file are documents and data that I think will help you to get a wider grasp of the organisation and its role. Do bear in mind that it is your professional knowledge and management skills that are required for the post. An understanding of the military aspect will follow once you have been appointed."

With a gentle chuckle, I said, "Appointed? I think that is a wee bit premature. Isn't there a preferred candidate from within the organisation?"

"Not that I am aware of," she replied. Then she added, "I would seriously encourage you to apply. SSAFA is at a crossroad. Two years ago, we appointed the Head of social work from outside of the organisation. She has now been promoted to the post of Director of the joint nursing and social work service. SSAFA now needs an experienced person to become the Head of its nursing service. I believe that we ought to recruit that person from outside of the organisation. I know that having two relatively new Directors at Central Office would cause anxiety amongst the health visitors but it is the right course for SSAFA to take at this time."

As with my appointment in Hampstead it appeared that the organisation was looking to recruit an outsider who was likely to bring a different experience and new ideas to the post. I was pleased that this informal interview had gone well. The hour had passed quickly. I now felt that I needed to spend some time in quiet reflection before taking any action. I thanked her for her time and encouragement. A week later I posted the completed application and waited for a response.

I was short-listed for an interview, and as a reference was required prior to my attendance, I had to notify my boss and colleagues.

"How could you? How could you?" asked Hannah, with strength of feeling that I had not heard her express before. Hannah, a Xhosa from South Africa, was a health visitor. "Some people don't know when they are happy," she grumbled as she walked towards the door.

."You are a traitor!" Those were the words of Holly, a health visitor whose father was a Naval Officer.

"What do you mean"? I asked.

"You are leaving us and the NHS to go to work for those people and that organisation? You must be out of your mind."

"And why shouldn't I?" I asked.

"Because, my dear friend, *you* do not know anything about the military. It is a male-dominated society that has been governed by rank, and privilege and you are female and black. You will be an easy pushover. They will chew you up and spit you out in a second. You won't even know it is happening. You will live to regret it. Mark my words."

"Oh, well!" I muttered. I was surprised at the forcefulness of her tone and language, and I began to wonder whether indeed I had misinterpreted the requirements of the post.

As the days went by, the staff became more accepting of the possibility that I could be appointed to the post. They got great pleasure from saluting whenever I entered their offices. Holly offered her advice. "Please do not wag that index finger of yours when you are answering questions at the interview. The military will not take kindly to that."

I laughed, for I was well known throughout the District for using that particular gesture. I promised to take heed of her advice.

Chapter 8:
Leading Change in SSAFA

I realised that I was about to enter another world when I received my letter inviting me to attend my interview. The letter was phrased in formal military language. It read: "You are required to attend the RAF Recruitment and Medical Screening Centre in High Holborn at nine thirty in the morning of the twenty-sixth of October, and then report to SSAFA Central Office for an interview at twelve noon precisely."

I bristled at the tone of the letter, but I reassured myself that, as this was the world of the military that I was preparing to enter, I would have to get accustomed to their use of the English language.

The medical examination continued my introduction to the military culture of SSAFA. The medical took place at the RAF Centre in High Holborn and was thorough. I underwent the examination that was routinely offered to personnel who were about to serve in the Royal Air Force. It seemed to last forever. I became anxious as the hands of the clock kept moving on towards midday and there were yet more tests to be completed. In the end, I asked the medical officer to inform SSAFA of the delay, as the examination was taking longer than had been anticipated. My interview was rescheduled for two o clock.

When I arrived at SSAFA Central Office, there were three other female candidates dressed in military uniforms who were waiting to be interviewed. I could not tell which service they belonged to as I could not differentiate between the Army, the Air Force, and the Navy.

My cheerful "Good afternoon" was met with blank stares and stony silence. I recognised my first snub and wondered whether it was the uniform that had endowed them with a feeling of superiority. I smiled inwardly and said to myself, That will teach you not to be familiar with nurses in military uniforms.

I pretended not to notice their surreptitious glances. I could tell that they were curious to find out what I was doing there. I thought I was wearing a smart civilian outfit, but as far as they were concerned I had fallen short of the dress code expected for the occasion. In the end, unable to contain her curiosity, one of the nurses, who was wearing a grey uniform, turned to me and said, "Excuse me. Are you here for the interview?"

"Yes," I replied.

My silent friends exchanged cynical glances, and no further words were spoken.

A few moments later, a tall, slender young woman entered and invited me to accompany her to SSAFA's Board room where the interview would take place. The room was intimidating. There was a long highly polished table that was wider than usual and created a distance between myself and the interviewers.

The room had large framed photographs of high-ranking officers in uniform and maps of the overseas Commands where the SSAFA Sisters were posted. But what I found even more intimidating than the wall hangings were the officials who were about to conduct the interview. There were seven people on the interview panel. I was introduced to Lady Kirby, Brigadier Warren, Air Commodore Francis, and Mr Smith, a member of the SSAFA Council. Then there was Mrs Clover, an independent assessor who had a nursing background and a gentleman who introduced himself as "The Controller". This was the title given to the Chief Executive of the Association.

Apart from the independent assessor and the Controller, everyone else wore uniforms that held no meaning to me. They sat on the opposite side of the table, their expressions inscrutable. Lady Kirby started the process, and smiling endearingly asked about my military experience.

Inwardly, I thought, You are fully aware that I do not have any military experience, so why are you trying to play a game with me?

But with what I hoped was an equally charming smile, I replied, "I cannot claim to have any experience of the military; however, I do believe that I possess the professional and managerial expertise that the post requires. And, if I were to be successful, I would look to SSAFA, who is aware of my military deficit, to facilitate my learning in that area."

Still smiling outwardly, Lady Kirby winced slightly at my response, then continued to pose further questions.

Next, it was the turn of Brigadier Warren who, in an upper-class English accent asked, "How would you increase the establishment in Germany?"

I thought that the question was about the provision of health services in Germany, and I replied, "As I have never been to Germany, my response would be a hypothetical one based on UK health policies."

To each of the answers that I gave to the Brigadier he responded with the words "Yaar, Yaar, Yaar" and, after the third such "yaar", I stopped, leant forward slightly, and with a smile and the wagging of my index finger, I said "I have a feeling that I am not answering the question as you would like me to."

"No," he said. "Would you like me to rephrase it?"

"Yes," I replied.

He rephrased his question.

"Ah," said I. "You want an answer based on health trends." So I replied by giving a more technical answer about the current statistics and thinking on infant mortality and morbidity rates within the NHS. This was the answer he sought. From the corner of my eyes, I could see the other panel members trying desperately to suppress their amusement at my response.

By the time I had answered all of the Brigadier's questions, I felt that I had lost whatever hope I had of being taken seriously for the post. I felt like a mouse that was being baited by a cat before it decided to pounce. But I was now fully engaged in the interview, and there was no honourable way out. I do not recall the questions posed by the other officers. Nor can I remember my responses. But there was a little voice inside that kept asking, What are you doing here? Why have you put yourself in this situation?

Holly's words and. those of Nurse Barton's came back clearly to haunt me.

Were they both right?

The interview had lasted for one hour. It was after three o'clock when it ended. I felt an unusual urge for a double gin and tonic. But this was 1982, and the pubs closed at three in the afternoon. So I bought cream cakes and returned to the Health Centre to be chastised and comforted by the health visitors.

An excited group of staff greeted me as I entered the health clinic. The first question they asked was "Did you use that index finger of yours?"

"Yes," I replied. "It was an involuntary reaction to a tricky question."

They laughed, and Holly said, "I am pleased about that, for it means that you won't be offered the post on the grounds that you intimidated an officer."

I was offered the post and I accepted it. The transition from civilian to military continued as I became one of the uniformed members of staff with an honorary rank of Colonel. I was issued with a smart grey uniform. This uniform was made to measure by Bernard Weatheralls of Savile Row and signified my position within the organisation.

One of the reasons for my appointment to SSAFA was to ensure that SSAFA nurses and health professionals built links with their colleagues in the NHS. They needed to update their skills, practices, and experience, and these links would help them to do that. I assumed that the staff would welcome these opportunities to improve their professional development.

My assumptions could not have been more misguided. Although I was received warmly by the administrative staff who worked at Central Office in London, it proved to be a very different matter where a number of the SSAFA Sisters were concerned. Whilst I received welcoming letters from senior members of staff in the various Commands; I was confounded by the telephone calls and the letters that were addressed to me from the field staff, expressing their reservation about my appointment as the Head of the service. There were two recurring questions: "How," they asked, "do you expect to manage the service, when you do not have a military background or an understanding of it?" And, "We do not come under the NHS. How is your NHS experience going to be relevant to us? We come under military law and are answerable only to the military."

Their question about my military background showed an obvious misunderstanding of why I had been appointed. I was appointed to bring my professional expertise and management experience to the service, not for my understanding of the military.

The second question gave me more cause for concern. Whilst the staff did have an obligation to adhere to the military rules, they were all registered as nurses with the United Kingdom Central Council (UKCC). The UKCC was their professional registration and regulatory body. If they did not comply with the rules of their regulator, they would lose their nursing status and would no longer be permitted to practice.

This was worrying, and I felt that I needed to meet with staff in order to clarify the misconception. The letters also made clear that they were questioning my credibility. They were expecting me to demonstrate my worth. They had come to a view that as we were two new managers at Central Office who had been recruited recently from outside the organisation; we could have little understanding of its culture and practices. They were feeling insecure. Belatedly, I had to acknowledge that the next few months were likely to be more difficult than I had expected.

I knew that I had to complete my orientation into the Association before I could address these challenges more directly.

My orientation took place in the UK and included a meeting with the Director General of the Army Medical Service – General Baldwin.

My predecessor and I were escorted to his office in High Holborn by one of his staff officers. He rose as we entered and greeted us.

General Baldwin was a tall slender-built man, who lent dignity to a well-fitted uniform. He had kindly brown eyes and hair that had receded at the crown but was greying at the temples. We sat in comfortable armchairs. In a gentle, refined tone of voice and with a smile, he asked, "I am somewhat intrigued – Can I ask what prompted you to apply to become the head of the SSAFA Nursing Service?"

I could understand why he would be intrigued by my decision to apply to SSAFA, and I replied, "There were really two reasons. Firstly, SSAFA's advertisement for a professional head of nursing was tempting. It was the type of challenge I felt that I needed. Secondly, it seemed a good idea to escape from the NHS whilst it is being restructured."

"Oh yes," he said. "I have been reading about the implementation of the Griffiths recommendation and its future management. A number of our recently retired officers have been appointed to senior posts in the new management structure. It is going to be an interesting time for the NHS. I suppose it is easier for SSAFA to recruit health visitors whilst this upheaval is taking place."

I found it very interesting that the NHS was appointing staff from the military to help it adapt to change at the very moment that the SSAFA Nursing Service were looking to appoint staff from the NHS to help them manage change. There was something ironical about this turn of events.

Our conversation continued as he asked me about my background prior to joining SSAFA. He asked, "Where did you say you've worked as a health visitor?"

I thought, I didn't say. But I replied, "I practiced in the East End of London and later managed services in Hampstead."

"Hampstead?" he repeated. "That is an affluent part of London. Do they need health visitors there?"

I had heard that question many times before. "Oh yes, indeed," I replied. "They are very aware that they do. And I guess in that respect, they are similar to military families abroad."

"Have you had many military families in your area?"

"No, we haven't."

He smiled as he said, "I thought not."

Having discussed my reasons for joining SSAFA and my background in health visiting we then proceeded to address the challenges in Germany. The General wanted to know whether my predecessor would be accompanying me on my journey to Germany.

""No, General," she replied "I shall be leaving SSAFA at the end of the week."

"It is a pity that a visit could not have been included as part of the orientation programme. I believe that it would have been most helpful." He then turned to me and asked, "I know that it is very early days, but apart from this strange environment, is there anything that you've found to be significantly different from the NHS?"

This offered a direct opportunity for me to share my concerns about the staffs' confusion of their professional accountability as nurses to the UKCC with their requirement to adhere to military law. I glanced at my colleague, not to seek her approval, but rather to indicate that I was about to say something controversial.

"I am pleased that you have asked that question. I am concerned about the number of SSAFA Sisters who seem to have confused their requirement to comply with military law with their obligation to update their professional skills in accordance with the requirements of their regulatory body, the UKCC. They believe that their military status makes them unaccountable to the UKCC."

He frowned and asked, "Is that so?"

"Yes, I have had letters from members of staff to that effect, and I am quite concerned."

"Mmmm... Have you got a plan in mind?"

"I do have an idea of what needs to be done, but I would like your guidance on the best approach."

"How can I help?"

"Once I have settled into my new post, I would like to organise a seminar and invite a representative from the UKCC to meet the staff in Germany. I am told that this would be setting a precedent."

He looked at my colleague for confirmation. She explained "We have never before had to invite a member of a civilian organisation to meet our staff in the Commands." And, looking at me, she added, "I believe that it would cause anxiety and unrest amongst the SSAFA Sisters, especially as there have been major administrative and management changes at Central Office within recent times."

No one spoke for a while. General Baldwin broke the silence. He then offered me his advice. "Brigadier Warren, the public health doctor who was a member of your interview panel is due to attend a meeting at our headquarters here in London. I shall ask him to explore the possibility of SSAFA organising a seminar in the Command. I shall let you have the decision after we have met."

"Thank you very much," I said with great relief.

As we left the General's office my colleague squeezed my arm and whispered, "Well done; you've made a good contact there. The General is a paediatrician by profession."

"A paediatrician in the Army?" I asked. I was surprised, as I had not thought that there would be much need for paediatricians in the military.

"Yes. And that, I believe, is why he has such an understanding of the work of the health visitors and the importance of the health visiting service. I feel sure that you will be able to rely on his support for the seminar to be held in Germany."

I closed my eyes and said a quiet prayer.

―――――――――――

It was six months into my appointment before I was finally able to visit Germany and the staff that were working there. It was my first experience of travelling with the military, and it was a unique one.

Travelling to Germany started with a train journey from St Pancras Station in London to Luton railway station. Here a bus was laid on for all military personnel and civilian family members to be taken to the airport. Once everyone was seated, the Corporal in charge stood at the front of the bus and delivered, in brusque military language, elementary instructions about what we were to do on entering the airport. I found this to be rather strange as there were senior officers and other seasoned travellers on board. Later, when I commented that I thought it odd for a Corporal to give instructions in that manner, I was told by one of the officers that, as many of the wives were young and inexperienced, the approach was a necessary one.

There were other unique rituals that formed part of the journey. At the check-in counter, a cream tag with a distinctive black mark was attached to my bag. I learnt sometime afterwards that it was used as a means to identify the baggage that belonged to the senior officers so that they would be given priority once the plane had landed.

It was when we eventually arrived at RAF Brugen that I felt the full impact of what it was like to work on a military base. There were men and women in uniforms everywhere. Some carried guns. No one smiled. They followed procedures as if programmed to do so. Respect for the rank of individuals was absolute.

As I made the journey from a civilian culture in the NHS to a military culture in SSAFA, I found myself having empathy for the SSAFA Sisters who had to live and work in this environment. In their attempt to integrate into the military system, it was easy for them to forget that they were civilian nurses, leading them to have a crisis of identity.

I was glad to finally arrive at my room in the Visitors' Mess. The room was very similar to the accommodation in a Travel Lodge and Motel. I was also looking forward to getting some rest before embarking on the busy schedule that had been organised for my five-day visit. But I had an important appointment before I could do so.

With a quick change into my uniform, I was ready to be briefed by the Military High Command at the Joint Headquarters in Rheindahlan. It was the first time that I was going to be wearing the uniform. Although I understood the reason why it was necessary to wear a uniform, I was ill at ease in it. I was a visiting civilian and not a part of the military. My uniform was a grey woollen suit with epilates. On these epilates were a SSAFA badge and two buttons. The badge and buttons were intended to signify my equivalent military rank of Colonel. This seemed to confuse the young soldiers who saluted as I walked by on my way to visit the Joint Headquarters building.

The Joint Headquarters was a long building that housed the Army at one end and the RAF at the other. A dimly lit corridor separated them. Each service had its own chain of command. I paid courtesy visits to both of them, where I had the opportunity to hear their opinion about the service that we provided.

There was a great deal to take in. I had to learn a lot of new terms and military abbreviations. I hoped that they did not notice the occasional glazing of my eyes.

This visit was followed by my first meeting with the SSAFA Sisters. I thought of some of the caustic letters that I had received when I was appointed, and I asked my senior manager what the staff's expectations were.

"They are really looking forward to meeting you," she said.

I looked at her over the rim of my glasses and replied, "Are they?"

We both laughed and she said, "Well, most of them."

Not all the members of staff were able to attend this meeting, but those who did looked extremely smart in their uniforms and gave an enthusiastic account of their roles. They described the distance they travelled in terms of hours on the autobahn rather than miles in the car. I began to appreciate the scale of the geographical area that they had to cover.

The health visitors wore uniforms with three SSAFA buttons on their epilates. This indicated that they had the honorary officer rank of Captain. I wanted to know how the non-officer families, or those they referred to as "other ranks", responded to them when they visited wearing the uniform, so I asked, "Does the wearing of your uniform act as a barrier when you visit the other ranks families in their homes?"

They gave some thought to my question before one of them responded by saying, "Occasionally a young mother who has recently arrived in the Command may be a little unsure about our role. But once we have explained who we are and what we do, they become less anxious and will often initiate a visit."

Then one of the health visitors asked, "Are you able to tell us of your plans for the service?"

I know that this question was of great concern, discussion, and debate amongst the staff, who were anxious that I was going to impose major changes to the way that they worked. "I have no plans in mind at present. I want to learn about the work you are doing and to listen to any suggestions that you would like to put forward that would improve the service."

This response seemed to provide some assurance and the atmosphere became less formal. I decided to broach the subject of their obligation to adhere to military law and their relationship with their nursing regulatory body, the UKCC. So I asked, "Is there a dilemma for you as health visitors having to adhere to military law and your obligation to conform to the UKCC rules and regulations?"

There was a long silence. Then a brave member of staff said, "We are not accountable to the UKCC as long as we are subjected to military law."

This was the question that had caused such consternation at my appointment, as there was a perception that I did not respect their special status. There was silence as I waited for others to endorse her statement. But, as this did not happen, I said, "I think that you will find that is not the case." Again there was silence. Then I continued, "Would you find it helpful if I were to invite someone from the UKCC to bring you up-to-date on what is happening about the changes to nurse registration?"

"Yes," replied a number of them in unison. And with a promise that I would make the necessary arrangements, the meeting was drawn to a close.

I was pleased with what I had learnt from the members of staff. I came to the conclusion at the end of the meeting that, overall, they were providing a good and equal service to the families.

I returned at the end of the week to Central Office in London full of thoughts and images that I found difficult to dispel. I knew that there was a great deal of work to be done. But I was also conscious that we had a dedicated team of health visitors who were committed to the work that they were doing, and the families were benefiting as a result. Any change that I intended to make would have to be introduced slowly and with sensitivity.

I decided to develop a customised training programme for staff as, unlike their colleagues in the NHS, they did not have easy access to professional updating. I felt that I needed to find a way to resolve this imbalance without disrupting the service. I decided to seek the assistance of the relevant professional bodies. Together we devised a tailor-made course that we planned to take to the Germany Command, where the majority of the staff were based.

Change did not happen overnight. But I secured the support of General Baldwin, the Director General of Army Medical Services, and Brigadier Warren, the director of public health in the Command. The brief orientation meeting that I had in Holborn with General Baldwin had proved to be extremely helpful.

One year after my appointment, one of the professional bodies, the Health Visitors Association, conducted a one-week, tailor-made refresher course in the Germany Command. Later, a one-day updating seminar by a representative from the UKCC was laid on for forty-eight members of staff. I was heartened to see their reaction. Some members admitted that their fears and anxieties were put to rest once they had the opportunity to listen to the presentation from the representative of the Nurses Registration Body. Most felt that the refresher course was going to enhance their future practice. Without exception, they expressed the wish to have further updating on a regular basis.

This was going to be costly for SSAFA. We decided that our best approach would be to establish our own In-service Training Centre in the Germany Command. The Centre would also be responsible for ensuring that staff in the far-flung Commands was included in the training. It was later extended to include updating courses for the SSAFA social workers.

Once again I discovered that by experimenting with something new and by adopting a flexible approach with colleagues, it was possible for them to adapt more readily to change.

Chapter 9:
Developing Health Services for Gurkha Families

One of the most interesting and rewarding challenges in my career was the development of health visiting services for the wives and children of the Gurkha soldiers. The Gurkha regiments are comprised of men from the hill tribes of Nepal. These Nepalese soldiers are renowned for their toughness and skill. For nearly two hundred years the Gurkhas have fought on the side of the British in almost all their major conflicts.

Their regiments served in Hong Kong and Brunei. Their family arrangements were different from those of UK soldiers. A Gurkha had to complete six years of active service and achieve a specific rank before he was given permission to be accompanied by his wife and children for a period of three years.

The MoD decided, in 1984, to change the healthcare arrangements for Ghurkha families. SSAFA was asked whether it would be prepared to establish a health visiting service for those families posted to the Command and also to Brunei. It was to be based along similar lines as that already provided for the British families. SSAFA agreed to explore the feasibility of doing so. I was excited at the idea of having to develop the new service and looked forward to the challenge.

Up until 1984, the Women's Royal Voluntary Service (WRVS) were responsible for providing support to the families. These women had spent many years with the Gurkha regiments and were very dedicated to their work.

The regiments were located in a part of Hong Kong known as the New Territories, and the volunteers lived with the Gurkha families in what was known as "Gurkha Family Lines". They moved with the regiments wherever and whenever they were posted. There was a strong link between the volunteers and the families. Their role was that of trusted friend and welfare worker.

I made my first visit to Hong Kong in January 1985. This visit had two objectives. Firstly, I needed to meet with the SSAFA health visitors to review the work that they were dong with the British families. Secondly, I had to hold discussions with the Brigadier of Gurkhas about the MoD's proposal for the new service to the Gurkha families. I was warned before leaving Central Office that the MoD's proposal would meet with strong resistance in Hong Kong.

The flight to Hong Kong seemed to take forever. I travelled on a military plane. The passengers were all service personnel and their families. Some were returning from a holiday in the UK. Others were about to join their regiment on their first posting to the Command. We had left Gatwick Airport at eight o'clock in the evening. With the pilot's skilful manoeuvring of the plane between the mountains and the skyscrapers and much to my relief, we landed safely at Kai Tak Airport at seven o'clock, local time, the following evening.

I stayed at HMS Tamar. This was not a naval ship. It was a unique building in the shape of an upturned gin bottle that was situated near the waterfront. The building served as the administrative headquarters and mess for naval and other military personnel and the civilians attached.

Following a troubled night's sleep spent wrestling with jetlag, I had my first meeting. I was accompanied by SSAFA's Head of nursing when I met with Brigadier Francis, Head of the Command. We discussed the service that the health visitors were providing for the British families. The Brigadier was a taller than average slender-built man with slightly stooping shoulders. He had friendly blue eyes and a square chin. He greeted us as we entered his office and asked me, "Is this your first visit to Hong Kong?"

"Yes," I replied and added, "The journey seemed never-ending and, from the window of the plane, I found the descent into the airport terrifying."

"It does appear to be like that on the first occasion, but it becomes less so the more times you do it. Did you have a good night's sleep? Most visitors to the Command get their GP to prescribe sleeping tablets before they embark on the journey."

"Sleeping tablets?" I repeated.

He looked surprised as he said, "It is a necessary evil, I am afraid. One needs to have a good night's sleep in order to function properly the next day. Jetlag has no mercy here; it is known to take hold of its victim in the early afternoon."

Smiling mischievously, and with a twinkle in his eyes he said to my colleague, "You should have warned her about this. I think that it would be advisable to have a shortened day. Shall we have coffee?" He dialled a number and a member of his staff appeared, took our orders, and returned later, bearing a tray of freshly brewed coffee and biscuits.

Brigadier Francis was full of praise for the professional health visiting work that the members of staff were doing. He mentioned in particular the extra support that they were offering the young wives who, being a long way from the United Kingdom, were desperately homesick. Brigadier Francis leant back in his chair and looked directly at me.

He said, "We are indeed very happy with the work of our SSAFA health visitors. It would be a great pity if the quality of the work that they are doing were to be reduced as a result of having to extend their role to include an additional service to the wives of our Gurkha soldiers."

That was how Brigadier Francis introduced the subject of the MoD's proposed new health visiting service to the families of Gurkha soldiers. As I did not respond immediately, he asked, "Were you aware of the MoD's plan? Were you involved in the discussions at Central Office?"

"Yes," I replied. "I was involved."

At this point we were joined by two civil servants who were representatives form the MoD in London. They had travelled on the same aircraft as I had done. Brigadier Francis welcomed them and introduced us. He explained the purpose of the meeting by stating, "The MoD has advised us that they intend to offer a health visiting service to the families of Gurkha soldiers serving in this Command and in Brunei. These good gentlemen are here to explain the rationale for this decision."

Turning to the representatives he added, "Perhaps you would like to brief us."

The senior of the two responded by saying, "The MoD will not be renewing the contracts of individual members of the WRVS when each one comes to an end. Instead it intends to offer these families a health visiting service similar to that being provided by SSAFA staff to British military families posted to Hong Kong and Brunei."

The Brigadier asked, "Is this a wise decision? The WRVS have looked after the Gurkha wives and children for many years and are very patient with them. They understand these young women. Most of them come from isolated hills in Nepal. They have no electricity and no running water. They need to be helped to cope with the different way of life in Hong Kong. When does the first WRVS contract come to an end?"

"In May of this year the contract ends for the WRVS serving with the Brigade of Gurkhas in Lymeun. The last contract ends in June 1986, and that will be for the WRVS who is attached to the Brigade in Perowne."

"May is only four months away. It does not give us much time. Is there room for negotiation?" asked the Brigadier.

"No, I am afraid not. We have been told to discuss the proposal with you and to return with initial plans for a smooth handover from the WRVS to the SSAFA health visitors."

Turning to SSAFA's head of service in the Command, the Brigadier asked, "Have you enough health visitors to take over the responsibility for the Gurkha families?"

Our Head of service looked to me for support, and I replied, "If SSAFA agrees to take over the service, I am sure that we would endeavour to meet the deadlines that are set."

The Brigadier remained thoughtful for a while, then said, "I think that you ought to visit the New Territories to be briefed by the officers in charge of the various Gurkha Regiments. You would also meet members of the WRVS at the Gurkha Family Lines. They will be able to describe the outstanding work that they do with the wives."

He rose and reached for a map of the Command. He pointed out the area covered by the New Territories. This was where the various Gurkha Brigades were positioned. It was a long way from Stanley

Fort, the Army Garrison where the British families were located. We examined the map. It was obvious from the widespread area that the present number of SSAFA health visitors could not be expected to take on the responsibility for the new service.

It was also clear that it would not be possible for us to visit the Regiments in the New Territories by road transport. The Brigadier arranged for a helicopter to be made available for us so that we could complete the mission in the limited time that we had. I realised that it would be a challenge to provide a health visiting service over such a vast geographical area, especially as the transport infrastructure was not the same as Germany with its autobahn networks.

The following days were spent visiting the various Gurkha regiments in the New Territories and holding discussions with the officers in charge. At each of the meetings, there was a Gurkha Major present. Each Major represented his particular regiment. These Majors sat very quietly and did not participate. It was not possible for us to know what each one was thinking; their facial expressions were unreadable

By the end of the week, we had visited all of the regiments and I had begun to form an idea of what would be required of the new service. A new team of health visitors would have to be recruited. The recruitment would need to be restricted to internal applicants, for they were familiar with the military environment and had an understanding of the relationship between SSAFA and the MoD. This was going to limit the number of potential applicants.

In addition, the new recruits would need private accommodation similar to that provided for the health visitors who worked with the British families. Unlike the WRVS, the accommodation would be away from the Gurkha Family Lines. I also realised that as the families were going to reside in the Command for a period of three years only and then return to their home in the hills of Nepal, the focus of the work would have to be different from the long-term health visiting that was offered to the British families. The Gurkha wives would have to be encouraged to take a more active role in the planning of their health education programmes and health promotion activities.

This was an intensive week in Hong Kong, with Sunday as my only day off. It was the most exhaustive visit to any of the Commands that I made during the time that I was in post. But by the end of the week we had devised a plan that we were able to take to SSAFA and the MoD.

Back in Central Office, we held further discussions with the MoD representatives to finalise the administrative arrangements. I decided that there were some certain considerations to be taken into account if the service were to benefit the families.

I felt that as we were about to embark on planning a new and hopefully effective programme of health promotion for the Gurkha wives and their children, it would be important for us to create an opportunity for our health visitors to learn more about Gurkha family structures and culture.

It was with this in mind that I approached the School of African and Oriental Studies and held discussions with one of the tutors, who agreed to develop a tailor-made Gurkha language course for the new recruits. The course would last for six weeks and would include an introduction to the culture, practices, and beliefs of the families.

The major challenge was finding the health visitors to take over the WRVS contract. We needed a team of eight to be trained in readiness to take up their post as soon as each contract ended. As we could only advertise internally this was going to be a constraint. Twelve applicants declared an interest. As we prepared to interview them, I was concerned that we would not be able to meet the four-month deadline of May when the Lymeun post became vacant.

It was at this point that fate intervened, and we had some good luck that enabled us to meet our May deadline. I can clearly recall a telephone conversation I had with a former SSAFA health visitor who wanted an appointment to see me about possible re-employment. She arrived as arranged a week later.

"Thank you for seeing me at such short notice," she said. "We have not met before. I used to be one of the health visitors in Germany when my husband was posted there. He has been posted back to the UK for the past three years, and I have been working as a health visitor in the NHS. I have kept in touch with friends in SSAFA, and they tell me that the service has improved."

"There have been some new developments," I replied.

"My husband has just received his posting orders for Hong Kong. He is due to leave in the next few weeks, and I was wondering if I could be placed on the books for relief or part-time work when we get there. I would like to keep up-to-date with health visiting as much as possible."

"Where is your husband being posted to in Hong Kong?" I asked.

"He has been posted to the Gurkha Regiment in Lymeun."

This was truly a fortuitous coincidence. My heart literally skipped a beat as I repeated, "Lymeun? "

"Yes," she said. "He is going to be in charge of the brigade there."

"We are looking to expand our service to include a health visiting one to Gurkha families when each of the WRVS contracts ends. Would you be interested in becoming our first health visitor to take up a post in Lymeun in May?"

She placed her hands on her cheeks and said with delight, "Yes, I would. I can't believe that this is happening; I really can't."

I gave her an application form and date for an interview. Two weeks later she was interviewed and appointed to the post. With her husband in charge of the Lymeun Brigade of Gurkhas, and with his support, she was going to be the ideal candidate to make a success of the changeover from the WRVS to SSAFA.

Her appointment meant that we were able to make a good start. SSAFA demonstrated that it was capable of providing a professional as well as a sensitive service to the Gurkha families. And, the Brigadier in charge of the Command became less anxious about the change from the WRVS to SSAFA health visitors

In 1997 Hong Kong was handed back to China. There is no longer a need for Gurkha Regiments to be deployed in the New Territories. SSAFA now has a presence in Nepal. The service continues in Brunei as part of the arrangement with the Brunei government.

I was pleased to have had the opportunity to take the lead in setting up this service for Gurkha families at a time when it was most needed.

1985 was a very busy year for Central Office. The year began with the journey to Hong Kong to arrange the transfer of Gurkha family health care services from the WRVS to SSAFA. It was also the year in which the organisation, celebrated its centenary. There was a full programme of events throughout the year. It began with a service at Westminster Abbey in February, and was followed a few weeks later by a conference in Berlin for the health visitors and social workers.

SSAFA was supported by the Queen Mother and Prince Michael of Kent. The Queen Mother was its Patron and Prince Michael of Kent its President.

As part of the year of celebration, The Queen Mother visited SSAFA Central Office and was given a guided tour of the building. We were dressed in uniform for the occasion. She showed a keen interest in the nursing service and commented on how difficult it must be to manage the service of such a far-flung Empire.

The conference in Berlin was officially opened by His Royal Highness Prince Michael of Kent. In recognition of the special occasion, the Controller and directors who worked at Central Office were invited to be his guests on the flight to Germany in the Queen's Andover. The Andover is smaller, more comfortable, and more luxurious than the military planes. Dining tables were laid for breakfast, and there were wardrobes for us to hang our coats. We were kept informed of the weather conditions throughout the flight, and we arrived in Germany unruffled and very much at ease.

The following day all the SSAFA staff, including those from the far-flung Commands, dressed in their best uniforms, boarded the Berliner en route to Berlin for the conference. The Berliner was the only British Military train in regular service in the world. We were told to remain seated when it stopped at Potsdam for its engine to be inspected by East German officers. The same applied when it arrived at Marienborn- the Russian check point where our documents were checked.

During my time in SSAFA, we managed to make some significant changes to the way in which the organisation delivered its services. As the years went by, SSAFA health visitors have welcomed and also initiated suggestions for improving the service. They became more aware of the changes in the health policy within the UK. They were keen to keep abreast with their NHS colleagues. We have been able to expand to include a community midwifery service. This was established initially in Germany and later in the far-flung Commands.

146

The managers also began to show an interest in the development of the general management structure within the NHS. They knew of a number of their ex–military colleagues who had been appointed to senior posts.

Management development became an important aspect of SSAFA's improved service. Our managers began to attend a management development course at Ashridge Management College. The college provided the training at a discounted rate as SSAFA was a voluntary charity. This was a great boost to the morale and confidence of the SSAFA health visiting managers, who in the past had not had the opportunity to develop their management skills at such a prestigious institution. We also made changes to the ways in which we promoted health in the various Commands. We created a Health Education Department, under the direction of a qualified Health Education Officer. This brought further improvement to our services. What was once SSAFA Nursing Service has become the SSAFA Health and Social Service (SH&SS), with health professionals and social workers working together in primary healthcare and social service teams.

It was in November 1989 that I made what was to be my last visit to the Germany Command to review the Community Health Service. Accompanied by the head of the SSAFA service, I visited every garrison where the health visitors were working.

This was the period of Glasnost, when the relationship between the West and the Soviet Union showed signs of greater harmony. I felt that this was likely to have an impact on the number of community health staff that would be required in the future. I had anticipated that there would be a reduction in the number of military personnel in the Command. And I had expected the subject to be raised by the Garrison Commanders during my visit. But it was never discussed.

During my last visit to the Headquarters in Berlin I asked, "Now that the relationship between the West and the Soviet Union has improved, are there plans to reduce the number of families who would be posted to the Command in the future?"

"Oh, no," the General had replied emphatically "That does not affect our operations in the Command. We will continue to require the good services of our SSAFA health visitors."

I still had my niggling doubts, but I accepted his reassurance. At the end of the fortnight's review of the service, I returned to my office in London. And one week later, the Berlin Wall came down.

I believe that SSAFA's Community Health and Social Work service is an example of how a collaborative and cooperative approach can lead to a seamless service that benefits families. The SSAFA Overseas Community Health and Social Services have a lot of experience and wisdom to share with the UK-based NHS

Back in London, SSAFA had sold its property in Queen Anne's Gate and had acquired alternative larger accommodation at Tower Bridge. This seemed to be an appropriate time for me to move on. It was now seven years since I had joined the organisation on a two-year contract

It was while I was in Berlin that I received a telephone call advising me that I had been appointed to the post of Nursing Officer in the Nursing Policy Division of the Department of Health. Another change of career and a new way of working were on the horizon.

So it was that in February 1990, I joined the Nursing Division of the Department of Health and became a Civil Servant. The Nursing Division, at that time, was divided into three "Groups" – Policy Group, Regional Liaison Group, and Education and Planning. I became a member of the Policy Group. We were responsible for the development of policy on discrete subject areas. I had to contribute to the development of the policy on nutrition, smoking, sexual health, family planning, women's health, ethnic minority health, health promotion, and vaccination and immunisation. It was not an easy task to keep abreast with all these areas, for there were occasions when the dates and times of meetings coincided, and I had to resort to providing a written response.

There were also times when I was impatient to see end results. I had to remind myself that this was a policy-development post, and that this is a slow process. The pace was slow because of the need to consult as widely as possible. In addition, we had to ensure that we had taken account of the contribution of the professional organisations and wider interest groups before we could attempt to write a preliminary draft and begin the circulation process for comments.

Although this way of operating was both interesting and stimulating, and I had the opportunity to meet and to work with experts in the various fields, I did not achieve the level of job satisfaction that I had done when I managed health services in the NHS and SSAFA.

I had been working in the Department of Health for three years when I was contacted by the Branch of the Departmentt that was responsible for market testing. Market testing, or assessing and measuring ways in which services could improve their quality, efficiency, and effectiveness had just been introduced to the NHS. The Head of the Branch telephoned and introduced himself, "Shirla," he said, "I have been told that you have had experience of working for the Ministry of Defence."

"No, I have not worked for the MoD," I replied. "I was employed by the Soldiers, Sailors, Airmen and Families Association to run their Overseas Community Health Services."

"Well, in my books that is the same as the MoD," he said jokingly.

"Can I ask the reason for the question?"

"We have just been approached by the Germany Command, who has been told that it has to market test the Army health services, with a view to saving approximately eighteen million pounds."

"Oh," said I, "that sounds interesting."

"I hoped you might say that." Then he added "The military presence in the Command is to be reduced significantly. As a result their medical service will have to be reconfigured. The Command has set up a small market testing team to undertake the project, and the MoD is asking for some one from the Department of Health to join the team as an advisor. This would be for a period of six months. One of your nursing colleagues mentioned that you had run and managed health services over there and suggested that I should ask you if you would be interested."

I thought, So, I was correct when, in 1989, on my last visit to that Command as the head of the SSAFA Community Health Service, I had raised the subject of a possible reduction in military personnel with the General in Berlin.

But I replied, "I don't know anything about market testing. Isn't there someone from your branch who would like to go?"

"There are not many of us here, and we cannot afford to second anyone for that length of time. We would be prepared to give our support to you if you decided to accept."

"I must say it sounds very interesting, but I would rather like to think about it and perhaps come over to see you at your office to discuss it further before I make a commitment."

He seemed delighted with the suggestion, and we arranged a time that was convenient for us to meet. We met later that week, and I agreed to visit the Command to meet with the project team leader to find out more about what would be entailed. I flew from RAF Northolt on the military flight one afternoon, and I met with the team the following day. They were all Lieutenant Colonels. The team leader was a Royal Engineer; there was a public health doctor, a senior medical officer, and a dentist. There was something about this team that appealed to me. They were dedicated and seemed excited about the challenge. They were frank about the difficulties and obstacles that they were likely to encounter.

Over the next few days I gave the offer a great deal of thought. I felt that a six-months secondment to work with this group would be not only stimulating, but enjoyable. I decided to accept the offer to act as the Department of Health's Advisor to the Project Group. And, in May 1994 I joined the team in the Germany Command.

When we were more than four months into the project, the MoD decided to widen the market testing exercise to include the service that was provided by the Royal Air Force. The time had to be extended so that they could be brought up to speed. I agreed to remain as the Advisor for the extended period.

Each member of the team had a specific role. Along with my advisory role, I undertook to oversee the specification for the nursing, midwifery, and health visiting aspects of the service. In that way, I made sure that it complied with the UKCC regulations, code of conduct, and standards of practice. I had to consult with colleagues and professional bodies in the UK on the rules and regulations as they applied to the various branches of the profession. It was a most interesting and challenging exercise that lasted a total of eighteen months.

As the project was coming to an end, I had time to reflect. I felt that I had been privileged to have had such a varied career in the NHS. It was also at this time that the Department of Health was offering its staff the opportunity to take what was termed "A voluntary early retirement settlement". A number of my nursing officer colleagues had decided to apply, and I did likewise. So it was that three months after the end of the market testing project, I retired from both the civil service and the health service.

Two years after my retirement, the NHS celebrated its fiftieth anniversary. As part of the arrangements for the celebration, a survey was undertaken to find the names of fifty women whom it was felt had made a significant contribution to the work of the National Health Service.

I was unaware that such a survey had taken place. So, I was surprised but pleased when I was informed that my name had been put forward and that I was to be included amongst the fifty women.

I was asked who had impressed me most in my career. This gave me an opportunity to reflect on the many inspiring people that I had met during my working life. There were dozens of inspiring people; in the end I chose two.

Miss Gilian Pittom, who was the head of the Community Health Service in Waltham Forest at the time when I was employed as a health visitor, and who encouraged me to undertake my first management course, and the late Mrs Kate Conway Nicholls, the Divisional Nursing Officer of the Hampstead Health Authority, who appointed me to my first management post and had offered me invaluable mentorship – something that was unknown at the time.

In 2000 I was awarded membership of the Order of the British Empire for service to Nursing Leadership. This was another pleasant surprise to receive such recognition and to realise that my colleagues and others had valued the work that I had completed during my time in the NHS.

My Native Land

The clocks no longer chime;
Church bells no longer ring.
The village now stands still
For silence, like a creeping vine,
Has robbed it of its will.

Where once in fields young children roamed
And yellow buttercups bloomed,
Parched earth, loose sand, and stunted palms
Have changed what was our home.

Strong winds and tropical hurricanes
Swirl ferociously over the land.
Heavy clouds, like dark curtains,
Obscure the willing sun.

The seagulls, they have vanished
To another land.
Deserted palms and grape trees
Cast their shadows on the sand.

But the relentless waves of the Atlantic
Continue to thrash the shore,
Denuding stones and boulders
Until they are no more.

Printed in the United States
132076LV00007B/165/P